Plays of Black Americans

Plays of
Black Americans

New Expanded Edition

The black experience
in America, dramatized
for young people

Edited by SYLVIA E. KAMERMAN

Publishers   PLAYS, INC.   *Boston*

Library of Congress Cataloging-in-Publication Data

Plays of Black Americans : episodes from the black experience in
  America, dramatized for young people / edited by Sylvia E.
  Kamerman.
     p. cm.
  Summary: A collection of plays reflecting the black experience
in America.
  ISBN 0-8238-0301-5 (pbk.)
  1. Children's plays, American--Afro-American authors. 2. Afro-
Americans--Juvenile drama. 3. American drama--20th century.
[1. Plays. 2. Afro-Americans--Drama.] I. Kamerman, Sylvia E.
PS627.N4P55   1994
812'.540809282'08996073--dc20   94-9314
                                          CIP

Manufactured in Canada

Contents

Plays of Black Americans

Freedom Train

by Craig Sodaro

Characters

LAURA CAMPBELL, *14*
JESSIE CAMPBELL, *her sister, 12*
MARY CAMPBELL, *their mother*
LEVI CAMPBELL, *their father*
ANNIE, *a "conductor"*
OLD NED, *slave*
TEDDY, *his grandson, 8*
BIRDIE, *his granddaughter, 10*
JACK NELSON, *slave catcher*
SHERIFF HARDCASTLE

TIME: *A stormy night in 1851.*
SETTING: *The Campbell Grocery and Dry Goods Store in an Ohio river town. Long counter center has scales, sacks of sugar, boxes of thread, and bolts of material on it. Shelves behind counter are stocked with canned goods, blankets, and household supplies. In front of counter are sacks of flour and a barrel. Hams hang from hooks above counter. Table and two chairs are down right. Window with shade or curtain is left. Lantern hangs on wall, right. Wing entrances are right and left, right leading to rest of house, left leading outside.*

AT RISE: LAURA CAMPBELL *sweeps floor.* JESSIE CAMP-
BELL *looks out window.*

LAURA: Jessie, stop looking out the window. You'll make
folks suspicious.

JESSIE: Nobody's out tonight in this weather. Besides,
I'm scared. What if we get caught?

LAURA (*Firmly*): We won't. (*As* JESSIE *takes blankets
from shelf,* MARY CAMPBELL *comes out from under
counter.*)

MARY: I think this will work just fine! We can put these
flour sacks over the trap door.

LAURA: Pa will be surprised when he sees the counter
over here.

JESSIE (*Fearfully*): He'll know exactly what we did.

MARY: But it will be over and done with. Besides, I
know deep down he would help . . . if he could.

LAURA: Are you sure?

MARY: Your Pa always does what's right, Laura. I am
glad, though, that he's had to help your uncle with
the calving. He won't be back for at least two days,
and by then they'll be gone.

JESSIE: Here are some blankets, Ma.

MARY: Good. And we have plenty of bacon and bread in
the cellar to fill their haversacks. I'm sure they'll be
hungry and tired when they arrive.

LAURA: When will they get here? (LAURA *moves to
window.*)

MARY: I have no idea.

LAURA (*Nervously*): Ma, someone's coming!

MARY: Now, remember, girls, these people are to be
treated as our guests. We must be courteous and hos-
pitable. (LEVI CAMPBELL *enters, wearing hat and
rain slicker.*) Levi! We didn't expect you for another
two days!

LEVI (*Removing hat and slicker*): It's not fit for a man or beast out there!

LAURA (*Tentatively*): Welcome home, Pa!

LEVI (*Fondly*): It's good to be home. Mother Nature worked much faster than we anticipated and all the calves were born.

MARY: (Sit and rest yourself, Levi. I'll fetch you a cup of coffee. (Mary, *nervously glancing at* LAURA *and* JESSIE, *exits right.* LEVI *sits at table.*)

JESSIE: How is Uncle Peter?

LEVI: As grouchy as ever. I wish he would join us here in the city. He worries too much about the weather. (*Looks around*) It looks as if you three have been moving things around here. (*He indicates counter.*)

LAURA: Yes, we have.

LEVI: It must have been hard to move the counter over the trap door.

JESSIE: Oh, it wasn't that hard. (MARY *enters with mug.*)

LEVI (*Suspiciously*): Mary, change for a reason is fine. Change without reason raises suspicions.

MARY: We have our reasons, Levi.

LEVI (*Tensely*): I see. We've been over all this, haven't we?

MARY: I know, but—

LEVI: You know, of course, it is a crime to hide fugitive slaves. . . .

MARY: Yes, but—

LEVI (*Rising; sternly*): If we are caught breaking the law, regardless what you think of the law, we will lose our livelihood. Then what will we do? Become fugitives ourselves?

JESSIE (*Firmly*): But, Pa, slavery is wrong.

LEVI (*Defensively*): There is no slavery in Ohio.

LAURA: You know what Jessie means, Pa. It's wrong anywhere.

LEVI: We aren't responsible for what the people in other states do.

MARY (*Picking up lantern and lighting it*): You heard Reverend Pettibone say our country is like a body, Levi. If an arm is hurt or sick, the rest of the body won't take care of itself. If part of it is sick, the entire body will become sick and die. (MARY *exits left.*)

LEVI (*Calling after her*): Where are you going, Mary? What are you doing? (MARY *returns, without lantern.*)

MARY: It's a signal. The light hanging by the door will let the conductor know that this is the station. (*She pulls window shade down.*)

LEVI (*Alarmed*): Conductor? Station? What are you talking about?

LAURA: You know—a station on the Underground Railroad, Pa.

JESSIE (*Excitedly*): We are one of the stations now!

LEVI (*Sitting at table; upset*): This will ruin us!

MARY: Reverend Pettibone asked if we could help out because slave catchers have been watching his place too closely.

LEVI (*Banging fist on table*): I won't have it!

LAURA: But, Pa!

LEVI: I have worked hard for what we have! I cannot risk everything to help fugitives from justice.

MARY (*Hotly*): Justice? Since when is it just for men to buy and sell other human beings? Is it just to sell children? Is it just to beat innocent people, or to refuse to teach children to read?

LEVI: When those people arrive, you tell them to go elsewhere, you hear? (*Knock is heard off left.*)

MARY (*After a slight pause; firmly*): You'll have to tell them yourself. (MARY *exits left. In a moment she re-enters, leading* ANNIE, TEDDY, OLD NED, *and* BIRDIE. *They all carry small satchels, except* TEDDY, WHO HAS HIS THINGS WRAPPED IN AN OLD PRINT SHIRT. THEY PLACE THEIR BUNDLES ON THE FLOOR.) Were you followed?

TEDDY: Nobody trailed us, ma'am, except a puppy.

ANNIE (*Proudly):* I'm a mighty careful conductor, ma'am, though the slave catchers are getting pretty crafty . . . especially now that they're getting paid so much to bring folks like these back to their masters.

BIRDIE (*Fearfully*): I don't want to go back!

OLD NED (*Comfortingly*): Now, Birdie, we aren't going back. I made myself a promise a long time ago to die a free man. And I'm keeping that promise.

TEDDY (*Proudly*): Me, too! It's freedom or die!

ANNIE (*With spirit*): Nobody's going to die on me, Teddy. In all my trips as a conductor I've never lost a passenger. We're in Ohio now, so the worst part of the journey's over. Folks here want to help you. (*To* LEVI) We're mighty grateful to you, sir!

LEVI (*Nervously, after a tense pause*): Ah . . . sit down. My daughters Laura and Jessie will fetch some stew for you. (*He looks at them.*)

LAURA (*Happily*): Yes, Pa!

JESSIE: Four stews, coming right up! (JESSIE *and* LAURA *exit right.*)

ANNIE (*Sitting at table*): From the sound of things, the slave catchers have been watching Reverend Pettibone's house.

MARY: He found a slave catcher lurking outside the parsonage, and recognized him as an ex-convict who had been in prison for robbery and assault.

OLD NED (*Sitting at table*): And how else can a convict make a living but chasing down runaways?

BIRDIE: My friend Tooley told me if we get caught by a slave catcher we'll be whipped like cream and beaten like eggs.

TEDDY: I won't let anything happen to you, Birdie.

LEVI (*Tentatively*): Don't worry. We'll make sure you're safe.

MARY: You'll spend the night in the cellar. The trap door is under the counter, and it's covered with a false floor. Even if someone should come looking, they won't be able to tell there's a trap door under it.

LEVI: It isn't the warmest place. . .

MARY (*Picking up blankets*): But it is dry, and we've got a blanket for each of you. Diggs Malone will be around tomorrow at dawn with his wagon. It's got a false bottom, so you can be taken to the next Station without fear of discovery.

ANNIE: Oh, that Diggs is a good man. It's not a comfortable ride, but it's safe. (LAURA *and* JESSIE *enter right with four mugs and spoons, which they serve to others.*) This smells delicious!

LAURA: It's Mother's famous recipe.

OLD NED: A bit of heaven, ma'am! (*Starts to eat*)

TEDDY (*Eating*): I'm so hungry. . .

BIRDIE (*Tasting stew*): I've never had anything like this before.

JESSIE: It's just plain stew.

OLD NED: We're used to rice, child—rice and bread. And I remember times when I was young like Birdie when I didn't get anything at all. That was the way I was kept in line.

LAURA (*Shocked*): Your Ma didn't feed you?

OLD NED (*Shaking his head*): My Ma? Oh, child. . .

ANNIE: At a very early age slaves are taken from their mothers. And most of them never know their fathers.

BIRDIE (*Brightly*): I remember seeing my mama once!

TEDDY (*Excitedly*): Me, too!

BIRDIE: She was the most beautiful woman in the whole world.

TEDDY: She brought us each a peppermint stick.

OLD NED: My daughter, Ruthie, walked ten miles each way to see her children . . . and she had to do that between sundown and sunup, because no master gives us time for visiting. 'Course, that was when she lived close. But then she was sold to a master miles and miles away. We haven't seen her in over two years.

BIRDIE: But Annie will find her and bring her to freedom, too.

ANNIE: I'll sure try, Birdie.

MARY: How many trips have you made on the Railroad, Miss Annie?

ANNIE (*Proudly*): This is my tenth, ma'am.

LAURA: Where are you all going?

OLD NED: Canada, miss.

ANNIE: There are colonies across the border where free men, women, and children are building new lives.

TEDDY (*Excitedly*): We're going to go to school!

BIRDIE: Annie says we'll learn to read!

LEVI (*To* ANNIE): It must take a great deal of courage to keep leading slaves to freedom when you know if you're caught you will end up a slave again.

ANNIE (*Firmly*): Again? Sir, I was never a slave! I was born a free woman, and I intend to stay a free woman.

MARY: So you risk—everything.

ANNIE: And if I didn't what would I be risking, then? Look at these two. (*She indicates* TEDDY *and* BIRDIE, *who are gobbling the stew.*) They're the future.

They're our hope. (*Loud knock is heard off left. Everyone freezes for a moment.* LAURA, *who is near window, peeks out.*)

OLD NED (*Nervously*): Folks sure shop late here in Ohio.

LEVI: It's not a customer.

LAURA: It's a man. He's holding his arm, as if it's hurt.

MARY: Get away from the window, Laura. (*To* ANNIE) This way. Quickly! (ANNIE *gathers up all satchels except* TEDDY'S. MARY *leads* ANNIE, OLD NED, TEDDY, *and* BIRDIE *behind the counter.*)

BIRDIE (*Fearfully*): We won't have to go back, will we? (MARY *ducks behind counter.*)

OLD NED: No, child!

ANNIE: They don't call me Lucky Annie for nothing! (*Slaves duck behind counter, out of sight.*)

MARY (*Rising*): The door is open. Climb down, quickly! (*Knock is heard again.*)

LEVI (*Moving left*): We're closed!

JACK NELSON (*Off left*): Open up! I need help!

JESSIE (*Worried*): Oh, Mother!

MARY: Laura, help me with this floor. (LAURA *ducks behind counter.*) Jessie, Levi . . . bring those flour sacks here. Cover the floor. (JESSIE *and* LEVI *drag sacks behind counter.*)

NELSON (*Off left; urgently*): Please help me! Open up! (MARY, JESSIE, LAURA, *and* LEVI *come out from behind counter.*)

MARY: Now, act natural. Laura, sweep. Jessie, clear the stew away. (LAURA *begins to sweep.* JESSIE *collects mugs.*)

NELSON (*Off left*): I've been hurt!

MARY: Open the door, Levi. (LEVI *exits left, reenters immediately with* NELSON, *dressed in a long coat and floppy hat. He holds his arm.*)

NELSON: I can't tell you how glad I was to find your light burning outside the door. Almost like a signal to travelers.

MARY: We . . . we just had some visitors.

LEVI: How did you get hurt? (NELSON *removes his coat. The sleeve of his shirt is bloody and torn.*)

NELSON: Caught myself on a nail sticking out from a fencepost. Tough to see details in this weather.

MARY (*Examining his arm*): There's quite a bit of blood. Sit down. (NELSON *sits, his coat across his lap.*)

LEVI: Let me hang your coat to dry.

NELSON (*Quickly*): Don't touch my coat! (*Others exchange puzzled looks.*)

LAURA: Shall I get some stew, Pa?

LEVI: Yes, I'm sure our guest is hungry. (LAURA *exits right.*)

MARY: Jessie, would you fetch me a pan of hot water? There's some on the stove.

JESSIE: Yes, Ma. (JESSIE *exits right.* MARY *goes behind counter and gets bandage.*)

LEVI: It's an odd time of night to be out working your way through fences.

NELSON: Not so odd in my line of work, sir.

LEVI: And what line of work is that?

NELSON: I find things. Things that have gotten lost.

MARY: Are you a lawman?

NELSON: Not exactly.

LEVI: What type of things do you find?

NELSON: Whatever people ask me to find. It's surprising how much men pay to get back what's theirs. (JESSIE *enters right with pan of water and cloth.* LAURA *follows with mug of stew, sets it down in front of* NELSON.)

LAURA: There you go, sir.

NELSON: Smells very good. Do you often cook stew at this time of night, ma'am? Seems to me you'd have eaten hours ago. (*He eats hungrily.*)

MARY: Didn't I mention we just had guests?

NELSON: So you did.

MARY (*As she wrings cloth out in water*): this will hurt a bit.

NELSON: (Don't mind that at all. (*She dabs cloth on NEL-SON's wound. He grimaces.*)

MARY: It's not much of a wound, really. Just a little scrape. (MARY *continues to clean the wound, then wraps* NELSON's *arm.*)

LEVI: That's good. A little wound won't detain you.

NELSON: You must not be in the habit of detaining people.

MARY: What do you mean?

NELSON: Your guests . . . I would have thought they'd stay the night.

LAURA (*Quickly*): Oh, they live close by.

NELSON (*Indicating* TEDDY's *pack*): Is that why they brought a pack all tied up?

MARY (*Worriedly*): Why, that doesn't belong to our guests.

JESSIE: It's mine. I keep my things in it.

NELSON: Let me see it, child.

LEVI: I don't see that it's your concern, sir.

NELSON (*Rising*): But it is. This country's got laws, see? And if a man is missing a piece of property, he can go after that property himself, or he can hire someone to go fetch his property back for him.

MARY: Property is one thing, sir. Human beings are another.

NELSON: Sometimes they're one and the same.

LEVI (*Firmly*): Sir, you've been bandaged and fed. Now, be on your way.

NELSON: But I have business here.

LEVI: We're closed for business.

NELSON: (*Rising, holding his coat tightly*): You think I'm a fool, don't you? But I'm not! I'm good at what I do!

MARY: And very thorough. You cut your own arm, didn't you?

NELSON: (I wasn't sure this was the new station on the so-called Underground Railroad, so I had to find some way to get in. But now I know. . . (*Prowling about room*)

LAURA: You don't know any such thing!

NELSON: that pack belongs to a slave as sure as I'm standing here. That's the very shirt I was warned to watch for. A Sunday shirt made of cotton. Just that pattern.

LEVI (*Shouting*): Get out!

NELSON: Not without my employer's property.

MARY: I'm sure your employer owns enough other property.

NELSON: He wants what's his! (*Stomps foot*)

LEVI: I'll tell you one last time. Get out!

NELSON (*In challenging tone*): Or what? You'll call the Sheriff? Should I remind you that the Fugitive Slave Law, passed just this year, guarantees that I have the right to capture and return my employer's property, even if Ohio is a free state? The Sheriff must obey the law! Now—where did you hide them? (*Stomps the floor*)

MARY (*Nervously*): Sir, we do not have any fugitives from justice under this roof!

NELSON: I think under the floor. . . (*Stomps again*)

LEVI (*Angrily*): There's nothing below but dirt.

NELSON: The sound is hollow. There's a cellar down there!

LAURA (*Nervously*): Just a crawl space.

JESSIE: (Barely big enough for a cat!

NELSON: We'll see about that! (*He draws pistol from inside his coat, which he drops.*)

LEVI (*Shocked, nervously*): We don't permit guns in this house!

NELSON (*Smiling*): If you're telling the truth, nobody will get hurt! (*He fires gun into floor.* JESSIE *and* LAURA *scream and run to* MARY. LEVI *grabs* NELSON, *and they scuffle.*)

MARY (*Frightened*): No! Stop that!

LAURA: Don't you hurt my father!

JESSIE: Stop it! Stop it! (NELSON STRIKES LEVI *with gun.* LEVI *crumples to the floor.* MARY, JESSIE, *and* LAURA *rush to* LEVI's *side, terrified.*) Pa!

MARY: Levi!

NELSON (*To* MARY, *angrily*): Bring them up here now! (MARY *goes behind counter. She moves flour sacks, false floor, and then opens trap door. One by one,* ANNIE, OLD NED, TEDDY, *and* BIRDIE *appear from behind counter. Meantime,* LAURA *and* JESSIE *help* LEVI *up.*)

MARY: Did any of you get hurt by the bullet?

ANNIE: No, ma'am. He hit the other corner of the room.

OLD NED (*Noticing* LEVI): What's happened?

NELSON: He'll be all right. that's what comes of aiding and abetting runaways!

BIRDIE (*Terrified*): I don't want to go back! I don't want to go back!

TEDDY: Sh-h-h, Birdie. It'll be all right.

OLD NED (*Somberly*): Don't tell her lies, Teddy. It won't be all right.

ANNIE: Ned, please!

OLD NED (*Angrily*): It won't be! Birdie's right! I don't

want to go back, either! (*Knock is heard off left.*)

NELSON: But you will! If my guess is right, that's the Sheriff. I told him a single gunshot would be the signal. Open the door, ma'am! (MARY *exits left.*)

ANNIE (*To* NELSON; *coldly*): Right now, while you're standing here so smug, there are ten trains full of passengers bound for freedom!

NELSON (*Sneering*): But this is one that got derailed! (MARY *leads* SHERIFF HARDCASTLE *on left.*) It's about time!

SHERIFF (*Unmoved*): So you found them, Nelson.

OLD NED (*Hugging* BIRDIE, *who is crying*): Don't worry, Birdie. I won't let them take you.

TEDDY (*Terrified*): Grandpa . . . I don't want anything to happen to you!

OLD NED: They'll split us up for sure now . . . and I can't bear that!

NELSON: You should have thought about that before you ran off! Let's go! (*No one moves.*) *Now*! (*To* SHERIFF) Sheriff, I demand you do your duty!

OLD NED: You're going to have to kill me first, Sheriff. I promised myself I would die a free man, and I'm keeping that promise.

SHERIFF: Now, see here, old man. The law's the law!

JESSIE (*Pleading*): It's a bad law!

LAURA (*Firmly*): You can't take them back!

LEVI (*Nervously*): Girls . . . be quiet!

SHERIFF (*To slaves*): Come along peacefully!

OLD NED: I can't do that, sir.

ANNIE (*Pleading*): Maybe there's someone who can help us, Ned!

NELSON: Move! (*Aims gun at* NED)

OLD NED: Pull the trigger, and I'm free!

BIRDIE (*Terrified*): Grandpa!

TEDDY (*To* NELSON; *frantically*): No, don't, mister!

NELSON (*Nervously*): I'm not going to tell you again, old man!

SHERIFF (*To* NELSON): Put that gun down, you fool! You won't collect a cent if he turns up dead!

NELSON: He's too old to be worth anything. But the others are valuable! Now, let's go! (SHERIFF, *standing behind* NELSON, *grabs ham from hook, hits* NELSON *on head.* NELSON *crumples to floor.*)

MARY: Thank goodness!

SHERIFF (*To* ANNIE): Get them out of here now!

ANNIE: Bless you, Sheriff! Bless you!

SHERIFF: Go quickly before he revives. (LAURA *and* JESSIE *give blankets to* OLD NED, TEDDY, *and* BIRDIE. TEDDY *picks up pack.*)

MARY (*To* ANNIE): Can you read?

ANNIE: Yes, ma'am!

MARY (*Scribbling on paper*): Here's where you'll find Diggs Malone. Maybe he can take you in his wagon tonight.

LEVI (*Nervously, glancing at* SHERIFF): Mary!

SHERIFF: It's all right, Mr. Campbell. There are those of us in authority who know injustice when we see it.

ANNIE (*Putting paper in her pocket*): Thank you!

MARY: Jessie . . . Laura . . . show our guests out the back way.

LAURA: Yes, Ma.

LEVI (*Behind counter*): Wait! (*He brings out peppermint sticks.*) These will give you some energy. (*Gives candy to* ANNIE, OLD NED, TEDDY, *and* BIRDIE)

BIRDIE: Thanks, sir!

TEDDY (*Licking candy*): Sure tastes good!

OLD NED: Nothing compared to the taste of freedom, Teddy. Nothing!

ANNIE: Let's hurry! Goodbye, and thank you all! (LAURA *leads* ANNIE, BIRDIE, TEDDY, *and* JESSIE *off right.*)

MARY (*As they exit*): You're going to make it! You'll be in Canada before you know it!

SHERIFF: There are stations all along the way. They'll do fine as long as they don't run into the likes of him again. (*Gestures to* NELSON)

LEVI: What are you going to do with him?

SHERIFF (*Wryly*): It's really a shame this ham fell on him accidentally. I hear tell, after a blow to the head, some folks imagine they've seen and heard things that weren't really there.

LEVI: Like fugitive slaves?

SHERIFF (*Shrugging, smiling*): I never saw one.

LEVI (*Smiling*): Neither did we—isn't that right, Mary?

MARY (*Worriedly*): But we'll be watched now.

SHERIFF (*Pointing to* NELSON): Not by this one. He fired his gun inside the city limits, disturbed the peace, and has been a general nuisance. With his record, he'll be very willing to leave the county for good, or be locked up for a long time.

LEVI: I'd hate to think this station had seen its last train arrive.

MARY (*Proudly*): I knew you wouldn't let us down, Levi.

LEVI: Mary, we'll keep that lantern lit as long as we have to—until *all* people are free. (*Curtain*)

THE END

PRODUCTION NOTES

FREEDOM TRAIN

Characters: 5 male; 5 female.

Playing Time: 25 minutes.

Properties: Mugs; spoons; various bundles or satchels of clothes, one wrapped in a patterned shirt; broom; bandages; pan of water with cloth; gun; ham; paper and pencil; peppermint sticks.

Costumes: 1850s period dress for all: long dresses for girls and women (Jessie and Laura also wear aprons or pinafores, Birdie and Annie wear capes). Shirts, pants, suspenders for Levi and Nelson; Levi wears rain slicker and hat when he first enters, Nelson coat and hat. Old coats and pants with patches for Old Ned and Teddy. Dark coat and hat for Sheriff.

Setting: Campbell Grocery and Dry Goods Store. Long counter center has scales, sugar sacks, boxes of thread, bolts of material on it. Flour sacks and a barrel sit in front of it. Hams hang from hooks above counter. Shelves behind counter hold canned goods, plates, blankets, etc. Table and two chairs are down right. Window with shade or curtain that can be closed is left. Lantern hangs on wall, right. Wing entrances are right and left, right leading to rest of house, left to outside.

Lighting: No special effects.

Sound: Knock on door; gunshot.

Langston Hughes:
Poet of the People
by Mary Satchell

Characters

LANGSTON HUGHES, *Black American writer*
MR. JAMES HUGHES, *his father*
SEÑORA GARCIA, *housekeeper*
THAD, *medical student*
WAITER
LONGSHOREMAN
YOUNG COUPLE ⎤
FOUR MEN ⎥
YOUNG WOMAN ⎬ *extras*
PASSERSBY ⎦
MRS. JONES
JOHNNY JONES
MRS. MARY MCLEOD BETHUNE, *Bethune-Cookman College founder*
HELEN, *her secretary*
ALICE JACKSON ⎤
JEAN BAXTER ⎬ *college students*
KEVIN DANIELS ⎦

SCENE 1

TIME: *Summer, 1920.*

SETTING: *Study in James Hughes's home near Mexico City. A desk, chair, and wastebasket are center. Accountant's ledger lies closed on edge of desk. Floor vase with tall pampas grass is nearby.*

AT RISE: LANGSTON HUGHES *sits writing at desk.* SEÑORA GARCIA *enters, holding feather duster.*

SEÑORA GARCIA: Señor Langston, how can you sit in one place for hours just writing?

LANGSTON (*Leaning back*): Señora Garcia, if I could spend my whole life writing, I'd be happy.

SEÑORA GARCIA (*Dusting vase*): You are a true artist, Señor Langston. (*Turns; sighs*) It is too bad that your father does not understand. You two belong to different worlds. You are a dreamer, and he is such a practical man.

LANGSTON (*Thoughtfully*): Father and I still don't know each other very well. (*Rises*) Since I arrived, he's been trying to make me into what *he* thinks I should be.

SEÑORA GARCIA (*Putting hands on hips*): I have been your father's housekeeper for a long time. Señor Hughes is a very stubborn man. But I'm sure he wants the best for you because you are *hijo querido*— his only son. (*Door slams off.* LANGSTON *and* SEÑORA GARCIA *turn.*)

LANGSTON (*Tensely*): That must be Father, and I haven't finished those accounting problems he left for me.

SEÑORA GARCIA (*Giving ledger to* LANGSTON): Quickly, Señor Langston! Take this ledger and give me those papers you've been writing on before your father sees them. He will be angry to find you have been writing poems. (*She sweeps papers into desk drawer, but one falls unnoticed to the floor.*)

LANGSTON (*Earnestly*): But, Señora Garcia, I can't be a make-believe son for my father any longer.

SEÑORA GARCIA (*Pushing* LANGSTON *into chair*): Señor Langston, if you don't do as I say, you had better brace yourself for a thunderstorm. (MR. HUGHES *enters, frowning.* SEÑORA GARCIA *turns with big smile.*) *Buenas dias,* Señor Hughes. We were not expecting you back from Toluca so soon.

MR. HUGHES: Hello, Señora Garcia. (*As he removes his poncho*) Langston?

LANGSTON (*Rising; uncomfortable*): Hello, Father. (MR. HUGHES *gives poncho to Señora Garcia, who exits with it.*)

MR. HUGHES: Well, Langston, let me see what progress you've made with the accounting problems.

LANGSTON (*Hesitantly*): Father, I need to talk to you.

MR. HUGHES (*Pointing to ledger*): We should go over the accounting problems first, and after dinner, we'll work on your Spanish lessons.

LANGSTON (*Pleading*): Father, please listen to me. . .

MR. HUGHES: We can talk later, son. Let me see your bookkeeping. If you're going to run this ranch someday, you'll have to learn how to keep accounts. (*Sits at desk*)

LANGSTON (*Giving ledger to* MR. HUGHES): I'm afraid I didn't get much done.

MR. HUGHES (*Slowly turning pages; irritated*): Langston, you've hardly done any work on these at all.

LANGSTON (*Pleading*): I tried—I really did. (*Sighs*) Accounting just isn't for me. I'm more interested in other things (*Paces*)—like writing.

MR. HUGHES (*Slamming ledger shut*): So—just as I thought. I suppose you've been sitting around here since I left— daydreaming?

LANGSTON: Actually, I've been very busy.

MR. HUGHES (*Angrily*): I didn't bring you to Mexico just to waste your life, Langston.

LANGSTON: I appreciate what you're doing for me, but—

MR. HUGHES (*Banging desk*): *No excuses!* You can be as successful as I am. (*Rises*) I left the States and moved here to Mexico because here a black man can live like any other man. That's why I insisted you move here from Cleveland . . . so you can have more opportunities! Here if he works hard, a man can be a success at whatever he wants.

LANGSTON (*Confidently*): I plan to be a successful writer.

MR. HUGHES: (Nonsense! You'll attend a good school and earn a degree in engineering.

LANGSTON (*Surprised*): Engineering?

MR. HUGHES: Of course. (*Proudly*) I can afford to send you to the finest schools in the world. (*Thoughtfully*) I hear there are excellent schools in Switzerland.

LANGSTON (*Stunned*): Switzerland! (*Agitated*) I don't want to go to school halfway around the world.

MR. HUGHES: All right, if you feel that strongly about it. Let's see. (*Thinks*) What are some schools with good engineering departments?

LANGSTON (*Eagerly*): What about Columbia?

MR. HUGHES: Columbia University in New York City?

LANGSTON: Yes. My grades were good in high school. I think Columbia would accept me.

MR. HUGHES (*Pleased*): That's more like it. Now, forget that silly writing business, and we'll see about getting you an application for Columbia. (SEÑORA GARCIA *enters.*)

SEÑORA GARCIA: Excuse me. Dinner is ready, Señor.

MR. HUGHES: We'll be right there. (*He turns, sees paper on floor.*) What's this?

LANGSTON (*Hurriedly*): It's nothing. I'll get it. (MR. HUGHES *picks up paper, glances at it, and frowns.*)

MR. HUGHES: Is this one of your poems?

LANGSTON (*Sheepishly*): Yes. (*Reaches for paper, but* MR. HUGHES *crumples it.*)

MR. HUGHES (*Sternly*): You won't have any more time for poetry. (*Drops paper into wastebasket and puts arm around* LANGSTON's *shoulders*) We'll talk later about what courses you'll take at Columbia University next year. You'll have to study a lot of science and math. (*They exit.* SEÑORA GARCIA *takes crumpled paper from wastebasket, smooths it out.*)

SEÑORA GARCIA (*Sadly*): Poor Señor Langston. Why can't his father just accept him the way he is? (*Puts paper in desk drawer and exits. Curtain*)

* * * * *

SCENE 2

TIME: *The next year.*

SETTING: *Langston's dormitory room at Columbia University. Bunk or twin beds and small bureau are upstage. Desk with papers, pencils, and books; two chairs; lamp, clock, and wastebasket are downstage. Closet door is in wall right. Exit is left. Large posters of Harlem street and café scenes are on wall upstage.*

AT RISE: THAD *sits at desk, reading.* LANGSTON *enters.*

LANGSTON: Hi, Thad. I don't suppose my father has shown up yet.

THAD: No, he hasn't, Lang, but if I were you, I'd get out of town before he arrives.

LANGSTON (*With a forced laugh*): You talk as if you've already met him. (*Sighs*) He's probably very angry with me now.

THAD: Can't say I blame him. (*Closes book*) Lang, what gives with you? All you've been doing lately is skipping classes and spending all your time uptown in Harlem. You haven't touched a book in weeks.

LANGSTON (*Placing jacket on chair*): I've tried to stick to my studies, Thad, but—(*Sighs*) my heart's just not in engineering.

THAD (*Rising*): Do you think I enjoy studying all the time? Sometimes I'd like to forget this (*Points to book*) and go uptown with you. (*Pauses; glances at posters*) It sure would be great to dig some jazz and just unwind for a while. (*He moves back to desk.*) But I want to earn a decent living someday. A medical degree is my ticket to a good life.

LANGSTON: I always thought you really wanted to be a doctor.

THAD: I *do* want to be a doctor.

LANGSTON: But you just said that a medical degree is a *ticket* to somewhere.

THAD (*Defensively*): It's a ticket to a comfortable home, a fine car, and all the other things I want in life.

LANGSTON (*Disappointed*): I thought a man decided to become a doctor in order to help people.

THAD (*Shrugging*): You're too idealistic, Lang.

LANGSTON (*Thoughtfully*): Maybe a better word would be *honest*. And speaking of honesty, I've decided it's time to tell my father the truth.

THAD: What are you going to tell him?

LANGSTON (*Earnestly*): That I just don't want to be an engineer. I came here to be near the Harlem scene, but I'm studying engineering only to please him.

THAD (*Putting hand on* LANGSTON's *shoulder*): You've got to be practical, Lang. An engineering career makes sense.

LANGSTON: For me, everything has to come from the
heart, or it's nothing. I want to write poems, stories,
and plays about black Americans. Harlem's where I
belong.

THAD (*Incredulously*): You'd give up a stable future to
spend your time in Harlem?

LANGSTON: Yes.

THAD (*Concerned*): But if you make a foolish decision
now. . .

LANGSTON (*Passionately*): At least I'll know I've been
true to myself.

THAD (*Embarrassed; looking at clock*): I have a biology
class soon. Your father will be here any minute.

LANGSTON (*Glumly; sitting*): I guess I'd better brace
myself for a storm. (THAD *gets jacket from closet and
picks up book.*)

THAD (*Trying to be cheerful*): Don't look so down, Lang.
Once you're into your engineerng courses, we'll both
laugh about the way you feel now.

LANGSTON: (I don't think so. (THAD *exits.* LANGSTON
picks up pencil and writes. Knocking is heard offstage. LANGSTON, *preoccupied, does not answer.
After a moment,* MR. HUGHES *enters.*)

MR. HUGHES (*Frowning*): Langston. (LANGSTON *looks
up.*) I hope you were too deep in your studies to hear
my knocking.

LANGSTON (*Rising*): Hello, Father. (*Uncomfortably*) I
know you're here because of my grades.

MR. HUGHES: I don't have to tell you how disappointed
I am. (*Sits*)

LANGSTON (*Sighing*): It's time for me to be honest with
you. When I came to Columbia, I tried to convince
myself that it was to earn a degree, but I really
wanted to get to Harlem.

MR. HUGHES (*Bewildered*): What's Harlem got to do with this?

LANGSTON: Everything. Thousands of black Americans live in Harlem, and I want to live with them. I have a burning desire to write about black people—our joys, sorrows . . . everything.

MR. HUGHES (*Irritably; rising*): Langston, are you telling me you want to drop out of Columbia?

LANGSTON (*Calmly*): Yes. Writing is the only future for me.

MR. HUGHES (*Angrily*): If you quit school, you won't get another red cent from me.

LANGSTON: It's not your money I need now, Father.

MR. HUGHES (*Softening*): Langston, I know I could never make up for all those years when you and your mother lived without me. But I tried to give you this opportunity—a ticket to success. (LANGSTON *shakes his head sadly.*)

LANGSTON: I have to strive for success in my own way.

MR. HUGHES: Is that your final decision?

LANGSTON: (*Quietly*): Yes, it is.

MR. HUGHES: Then I won't argue with you anymore. (*Puts on hat*) I'm returning to Mexico City on the morning train. (*Turns to exit*)

LANGSTON: Is that all you're going to say?

MR. HUGHES (*Turning back; sadly*): I wish you well, Langston, but I feel you're making a foolish mistake. I honestly have my doubts that you'll ever become a successful writer. (*Exits.* LANGSTON *moves to closet, takes out suitcase, puts it on bed. He moves to bureau and starts packing. Lights slowly fade. Curtain*)

*   *   *   *   *

SCENE 3

TIME: *Years later.*

SETTING: *Harlem street scene. Backdrop has painted storefronts: drugstore window showing table, chairs, and jukebox; barbershop with pole; doorway with steps and bench nearby. At right is pier with boxes and crates. At center, street light and sign mark intersection of Lenox Avenue and 125th Street. Chair, small table with cup and saucer and man's hat on it, are downstage.*

AT RISE: *Tableau of Harlem residents:* MAN *sits on steps at doorway;* YOUNG COUPLE *holds hands in drugstore window, sipping soda with two straws;* THREE MEN *stand beneath street light;* LONGSHOREMAN *works on pier. Spotlight comes up on* LANGSTON, *who sits at table, writing in journal.* WAITER *enters, moves to table.*

WAITER: Can I bring you anything else, Mr. Hughes?

LANGSTON (*Glancing up*): No thanks, Frank. You make the best coffee in Harlem, but I've had enough for one day (*Glances at wristwatch*) It's four o'clock already. I've been sitting here writing since noon. (*Rises*) I think I'll stretch my legs. (*Spotlight remains on* LANGSTON *during following monologue.*)

WAITER (*Smiling*): Suit yourself, Mr. Hughes. You're welcome at my place any time. (*Exits.* LANGSTON *places money on table, puts on hat, moves down center, carrying journal, then turns to audience.*)

LANGSTON: This is Harlem, my adopted home. (*Glances up, then turns back; with satisfaction*) It's a wonderful place. I've lived here for a long time, writing about the people. Young and old, they're my friends. Sometimes Harlem laughs, sings, and dances. (*Pensively*) Sometimes it's a struggle to survive. A lot of crying over broken dreams goes on in Harlem. (*Enthusiastically*) but whatever the situation, Harlem always teems with life. (*Gestures*) This is the Harlem of my poetry! (*Turns. Lights come up full. Other actors move naturally when* LANGSTON *walks upstage. He moves to* LONGSHOREMAN.)

LONGSHOREMAN: Hey there, Langston! Still writing your poems?

LANGSTON (*Nodding*): I can't seem to stop.

LONGSHOREMAN (*Glancing around; bewildered*): I don't see a thing here worth writing about. All I see are a polluted river and a lot of work for me to do.

LANGSTON (*Chuckling*): That's because you and I see things in different ways.

LONGSHOREMAN: (You may be right, Langston. (*Sighs*) I'd better get back to work. (*Waves*) See you around. (*Stacks boxes; lights fade to show* LONGSHOREMAN *working in silhouette; sound of foghorn and clanging bell. Spotlight on* LANGSTON *as he moves down to audience, recites "The Negro Speaks of Rivers."* At end of poem,* LONGSHOREMAN *exits. Lights come up.* YOUNG COUPLE *moves center, hand in hand. Lively jazz tune is heard.* LANGSTON *watches as they dance briefly, then exit. Music stops.* LANGSTON *moves center to recite "Juke Box Love Song."* THREE MEN *under streetlight begin to argue loudly.*)

MEN (*Ad lib*): Black people are treated in this country like second-class citizens, as if we don't belong! Now, just one minute! There are a lot of good things I can say about our country. Oh, yeah? Yeah! (*Etc. They turn to* LANGSTON.)

1ST MAN (*Pointing*): There's Langston Hughes. Let's find out what he thinks about America.

2ND MAN (*Beckoning*): Langston!

LANGSTON (*Moving nearer*): What's going on?

3RD MAN: We're having a little debate, and we'd like to get your opinion.

1ST MAN: What do you think about America, Langston?

2ND MAN: We know you're a poet of the people, so we respect what you have to say.

LANGSTON: Quite frankly, I love America.

3ND MAN (*Dubious*): You can't mean that!

LANGSTON: Yes, I do. (*Earnestly*) I've traveled to many places—Latin America, Europe, Africa, Russia, the Far East—but I wouldn't want to call any of them home.

1ST MAN (*To others*): See? Langston agrees with me.

3ND MAN (*Grudgingly*): Well, if Langston Hughes can say good things about America, I'd better think about it some more. (*Beckoning*) Let's go. (MEN *exit;* LANGSTON *moves down center to recite "I, Too, Sing America." YOUNG WOMAN enters, wearing red dress and carrying umbrella. Sound of jazz notes from saxophone is heard off. YOUNG WOMAN moves past* LANGSTON, *who smiles at her.*)

YOUNG WOMAN (*Flirting*): Hello, Langston.

LANGSTON (*Smitten*): Hello, Sue. You sure look pretty in that red dress.

YOUNG WOMAN (*Coyly*): Why, thank you. (*She walks away, glancing over her shoulder at* LANGSTON. *Jazz notes accompany* YOUNG WOMAN *off.* LANGSTON *recites "Harlem Night Song."* MAN *rises from steps and approaches* LANGSTON.)

MAN: I heard what you told those guys on the corner.

LANGSTON: You mean how I feel about America?

MAN: Yes.

LANGSTON: Do you agree with me?

MAN (*Shrugging*): Maybe I do. (*Pauses*) And maybe I

don't. (*Knowingly*) I can dig all jive, but I mind my business to stay alive. (*Pulls hat over his eyes and slowly exits.* LANGSTON *comes down center and recites* "*Motto.*" MRS. JONES *and* JOHNNY JONES, *carrying bag of groceries, enter.*)

MRS. JONES (*Cheerfully*): Good afternoon, Langston.

LANGSTON: Hello, Mrs. Jones. (*Puts hand on* JOHNNY'*s shoulder*) How's everything going, Johnny?

JOHNNY (*Morosely*): O.K., I guess.

LANGSTON (*Teasing*): Aren't you sure?

JOHNNY (*Irritably*): Sure, I am. Why are you so interested in me, anyway?

MRS. JONES (*Scolding*): That's no way to talk, Johnny. Apologize to Mr. Hughes.

JOHNNY: I'm sorry.

MRS. JONES: I don't know what's gotten into this boy lately. He should be happy because he was just hired for a job today.

JOHNNY (*Angrily*): Mr. Frank hired me to wash dishes in his coffee shop. How can you call that a job?

MRS. JONES: It's honest work.

JOHNNY: I don't want to wash dishes all my life, Ma. I want to go to college.

MRS. JONES (*Sighing*): I don't see how, Johnny. We just don't have that kind of money. (*To* LANGSTON) Langston, will you have supper with us on Sunday?

LANGSTON: I wish I could, Mrs. Jones, but I'm leaving town tomorrow.

MRS. JONES: Where are you off to this time?

LANGSTON: Mrs. Mary McLeod Bethune has invited me to visit her college in Florida. She wants me to read my poetry to her students.

JOHNNY (*Eagerly*): I wish I could go with you.

MRS. JONES: Maybe you'll go to college someday,

Johnny. But for now, your dreams will have to wait. (*Takes groceries*) Have a good trip, Langston. (*Exits*)

JOHNNY (*Sitting dejectedly*): My dreams always have to wait.

LANGSTON: Johnny, did you know I worked as a dishwasher in a little café in Paris?

JOHNNY (*Surprised*): *You* were a dishwasher?

LANGSTON (*Nodding*): I've also worked as a kitchen helper and cabin boy on a ship, and a farmhand in California. And those jobs were better than many others I've had.

JOHNNY: You probably didn't make much money.

LANGSTON: I made *very* little money in those days. But I always knew those jobs were just stepping stones to get me where I wanted to go.

JOHNNY: Where were you going?

LANGSTON: Toward my dream. After years of working, I earned a college degree and became a writer.

JOHNNY (*Rising*): You never lost your dream. (*Confidently*) Mr. Hughes, if you could do it, *I* can, too!

LANGSTON (*Clapping* JOHNNY *on shoulder*): that's the spirit, Johnny!

JOHNNY: I have to go home and help ma with dinner. Goodbye, Mr. Hughes. Say hello to Mrs. Bethune for me. (*Pauses*) And tell her that she just may be hearing from me one day. (*Exits.* LANGSTON *moves downstage to recite* "Harlem." *Lights begin to fade.* PASSERSBY *hurry past* LANGSTON *and call out greetings. He moves to table, down center.* WAITER *enters.*)

LANGSTON (*Taking off hat*): Could I have another pot of coffee, Frank?

WAITER: Sure thing, Mr. Hughes. What are you going to write about this time?

LANGSTON (*Gesturing*): Harlem, of course. What else?

WAITER (*Chuckling*): You'll always be our official poet, Mr. Hughes. You're really the poet of the people. (*Exits.* LANGSTON *sits, opens journal, writes. Curtain*)

*   *   *   *   *

SCENE 4

TIME: *Several days later.*

SETTING: *Bethune-Cookman College. Small bookcase, desk, and chair are left. Banner pinned to curtain reads,* BETHUNE-COOKMAN COLLEGE WELCOMES LANGSTON HUGHES.

BEFORE RISE: MRS. MARY McLEOD BETHUNE *sits reading at desk.* HELEN *enters right.*

HELEN: Mrs. Bethune, Langston Hughes just arrived.

MRS. BETHUNE (*Rising; pleased*): Wonderful! Please bring him in, Helen. (HELEN *exits;* MRS. BETHUNE *takes book from bookcase places it on desk. Anxiously, to herself*) I certainly hope Langston won't be angry when he discovers what I've done. (HELEN *reenters, followed by* LANGSTON. MRS. BETHUNE *greets* LANGSTON *heartily.*) Langston, I'm so happy to see you.

LANGSTON: It's a pleasure to visit your lovely campus again, Mrs. Bethune. (HELEN *exits.*)

MRS. BETHUNE: You're just the person we need now.

LANGSTON (*Puzzled*): Why do you say that?

MRS. BETHUNE: Our students need encouragement from someone who's become a success in spite of hard times.

LANGSTON: I haven't made a lot of money.

MRS. BETHUNE (*Waving hand*): Money's no true measure of success. Look at all the wonderful poems you've published. (*Pauses*) Sometimes, especially in moments of discouragement, I read your poems. They never fail to inspire me.

LANGSTON: I didn't think you ever felt discouraged.

MRS. BETHUNE (*Smiling*): Everyone needs a lift now and then.

LANGSTON: I wish I could reach more people with my poetry.

MRS. BETHUNE (*Suddenly*): Why, Langston, I should have thought of it before!

LANGSTON: Thought of what?

MRS. BETHUNE: I think you should travel around the country, reading your poetry. People need poetry, Langston; it would inspire them as it does me.

LANGSTON: If people are willing to listen, I'll be glad to read my poetry to them.

MRS. BETHUNE: Our students are certainly glad to have you here as their guest. (*Pauses, then mysteriously*) And speaking of guests, I've invited someone very special to enjoy your poetry.

LANGSTON (*Interested*): And who might that be?

MRS. BETHUNE: You'll find out soon enough. (*Picks up book*) Now, Langston. (*With a broad smile*) Would you please let me have your autograph?

LANGSTON: It's my pleasure. (*He signs book.*)

MRS. BETHUNE: I can't tell you what an important day this is for Bethune-Cookman College. The students are so looking forward to meeting you.

LANGSTON: And I'm looking forward to meeting them. (*They exit as curtain opens.*)

* * *

TIME: *A short time later.*

SETTING: *A high stool and lectern are at center.*

AT RISE: ALICE JACKSON, *carrying notebook,* JEAN BAXTER, *and* KEVIN DANIELS *enter left.*

ALICE (*Excitedly*): Isn't it wonderful? We're going to meet Langston Hughes!

JEAN: I love his poem "The Negro Speaks of Rivers."

KEVIN: And what about "Harlem Night Song." I hope he recites that one today.

ALICE: I can't wait to talk to him about poetry.

KEVIN: Alice, what makes you think Mr. Hughes would talk to you about his poetry?

ALICE: I don't want to talk to him about *his* poetry, Kevin. (*Proudly*) I intend to talk about *my* poems.

KEVIN: Are you serious? Why would a writer like Langston Hughes read your poems?

ALICE (*Lifting chin*): Maybe he'll laugh at me, but I'm going to ask him anyway.

JEAN (*Grabbing* KEVIN's *hand*): Let's get out of here before Alice makes herself look ridiculous. (*They exit quickly.* ALICE *moves to lectern, opens notebook.* LANGSTON *appears, unnoticed, stands right.*)

ALICE (*Bowing*): Thank you, ladies and gentlemen, for coming to hear me read my original poems. (LANGSTON *coughs;* ALICE *turns quickly in embarrassment.*) Oh, Mr. Hughes! I didn't know you were here!

LANGSTON (*Moving nearer*): I didn't meant to interrupt you. (*Gestures and sits*) Please continue.

ALICE (*Stammering*): I—I couldn't recite my poems to you. (*Pauses, then breathlessly*) But I must admit that I came early to ask you to look at my work and tell me what you think of it.

LANGSTON (*Earnestly*): Why do you want to write poetry, Miss—

ALICE: Jackson. Alice Jackson. (*Shrugs*) I just can't think of doing anything else.

LANGSTON (*Nodding*): I understand. May I see your work? (*She gives him notebook; he reads silently, then glances up.*) These are much better than my first poems. (*Rises*) You and I have something in common.

ALICE (*Wide-eyed*): We do?

LANGSTON: We both write from our hearts, and we believe in what we're doing.

ALICE (*Fervently*): At last, someone who understands! My friends didn't think you'd take me seriously.

LANGSTON: Sometimes the people we love don't understand or have faith in us.

ALICE (*Curiously*): Did someone you love ever try to discourage you?

LANGSTON (*Sadly*): Yes, Alice—my father. (*Wistfully*) We haven't seen each other in many years.

ALICE: Well, I'm sure things would be different if he could see you now.

LANGSTON (*Uncomfortably; looking at watch*): The program will begin soon, but I still have time to look at a few more of your poems. (LANGSTON *moves upstage;* JEAN *and* KEVIN *enter.*)

JEAN: Alice, we came to apologize. . . (*Sees* LANGSTON) It's Langston Hughes!

KEVIN: did you show him your poetry, Alice?

ALICE (*Smiling*): What do you think he's reading now?

JEAN: Really? That's wonderful!

ALICE: You were all wrong about him. (*To* LANGSTON) Mr. Hughes, I'd like you to meet my best friends, Jean Baxter and Kevin Daniels.

JEAN *and* KEVIN (*Awestruck; ad lib*): Pleased to meet you, Mr. Hughes. This is a real honor. (*Etc.*)

JEAN: We owe you an apology, Mr. Hughes. We thought you might hurt Alice's feelings.

LANGSTON: I've been hurt many times by people who said I couldn't write. But their doubts just made me work harder. (MRS. BETHUNE *enters.*)

MRS. BETHUNE: The students are beginning to assemble in the auditorium, Langston. Are you ready?

LANGSTON: Quite ready, Mrs. Bethune. (*Gives journal*

to ALICE) I've discovered a fellow poet here. She's very talented. (ALICE *beams.*)

MRS. BETHUNE (*Interested*): Is that so? (*To* ALICE) I'd like to hear more about your poetry. Why don't you and your friends join me and Langston for dinner after his program? (*Students ad lib thanks.*)

ALICE (*To* JEAN *and* KEVIN): Let's hurry so we can find seats down front. I don't want to miss a *word* of Mr. Hughes' poetry. (*Students exit.*)

MRS. BETHUNE: You've made this a very special day for that young lady.

LANGSTON: Today is special for me, too. I'm about to read my poetry in public for the first time. (HELEN *enters.*)

HELEN: Excuse me. Mrs. Bethune. Your other guest has just arrived. Should we come to the auditorium?

MRS. BETHUNE (*Quickly*): No, Helen, I'll go back to my office with you. (*To* LANGSTON) We'll start just as soon as I get back.

LANGSTON: All right, Mrs. Bethune. (MRS. BETHUNE *exits with* HELEN. LANGSTON *flips through pages.* MR. HUGHES *enters, carrying briefcase.*)

MR. HUGHES (*Hesitating*): Langston? (LANGSTON *turns, stunned.*)

LANGSTON: Father! (*Happily*) I can't believe it's really you! (*They move quickly to embrace.*)

MR. HUGHES (*Stepping back*): Let me look at you, Langston. (*Proudly*) Do you know, people I don't even know congratulate me and say what a lucky man I am when they find out that you're my son.

LANGSTON: How did you know I'd be here?

MR. HUGHES (*Chuckling*): Mrs. Bethune called me. (*Sincerely*) I've wanted to get in touch with you, but

I was ashamed—after the way I left when you needed me most.

LANGSTON: That doesn't matter any more. I'm just glad you're here.

MR. HUGHES: Then, you forgive me?

LANGSTON: Of course. . . . I inherited your strong will. I guess that's why I could never let go of my dream.

MR. HUGHES: Your writing touches people's hearts, Langston. (*Opens briefcase, takes out several books*) I have all of your poetry books—and your plays, novels, essays. . . Would you autograph them for me?

LANGSTON (*Happily*): I'd be glad to.

MR. HUGHES: Wonderful! (MRS. BETHUNE *enters.*)

MRS. BETHUNE (*Relieved*): There you are! I didn't know what to think when I didn't find you in my office.

MR. HUGHES (*Apologetically*): Forgive me, Mrs. Bethune. I couldn't wait to see Langston, so I asked some students to show me how to get here.

LANGSTON (*To* MRS. BETHUNE; *knowingly*): So, my father is that very special guest.

MRS. BETHUNE: I've been planning this surprise for weeks, Langston.

LANGSTON: I can't thank you enough, Mrs. Bethune.

MRS. BETHUNE (*Beaming*): Well, shall we begin the program?

LANGSTON (*Eagerly*): Yes, You may open the curtains. (MRS. BETHUNE *exits.*)

MR. HUGHES: I'd better hurry and get a front-row seat.

LANGSTON: Fine. See you after the program. (MR. HUGHES *exits;* LANGSTON *turns.*) My dream of making my father proud of me has finally come true. (*Thoughtfully*) Now I know the real meaning of success. (*Enthusiastically*) I'm going to take Mrs. Bethune's advice and travel all over this great country. (*Moves to lectern and faces audience*) I'll visit schools, churches, and community groups, and share the message of my poetry (*Gestures expansively*) with the people of America! (*Opens journal as if to begin program. Curtain*)

THE END

PRODUCTION NOTES

LANGSTON HUGHES: POET OF THE PEOPLE

Characters: 12 male; 8 female; at least 8 male and female for passersby.

Playing Time: 30 minutes.

Costumes: Scene 1, Mexican dress of the early 1920s: James Hughes wears poncho; Señora Garcia, long dress and apron. Scene 2, Langston wears jacket at opening of scene; Mr. Hughes, hat. Scenes 3 and 4, 1930s: Langston wears suit, wristwatch; Waiter, uniform; Longshoreman, work clothes; Young woman, red dress. Others wear costumes appropriate for the period.

Properties: Feather duster; suitcase; soda glass with two straws; journal; paper money; umbrella; bag of groceries; notebook; briefcase holding books.

Setting: Scene 1: James Hughes's home near Mexico City. Desk, chair, wastebasket are center. Accountant's ledger lies closed on desk. Floor vase with tall pampas grass is nearby. Scene 2: Dormitory room, Columbia University. Bunk or twin beds and bureau are upstage. Downstage, desk with papers, pencils, books; two chairs; lamp, clock, wastebasket. Closet door in wall right. Exit left. Posters of Harlem street and cafés scenes on wall upstage. Scene 3: Harlem street scene. Backdrop has painted storefronts: drugstore window showing table, chairs, jukebox; barbershop with pole; doorway with steps and bench nearby. At right, pier with boxes and crates. Center, sign marks intersection of Lenox Avenue and 125th Street. Downstage, chair, small table with cup and saucer and man's hat on it. Scene 4: Bethune-Cookman College. Bookcase, desk, chair. At Rise, high stool and lectern.

Lighting: Lights fade at end of Scene 2; spotlight in Scene 3.

Sound: Door slamming; knock on door; foghorn; clanging bell; lively jazz.

*This and other poems recited in this scene may be found in *Selected Poems of Langston Hughes* (Alfred A. Knopf, 1988).

George Washington Carver

by Mildred Hark and Noel McQueen

Characters

GEORGE, *George Washington Carver as a boy*
AUNT SUE CARVER
UNCLE MOSE CARVER
MARTHA
GEORGE WASHINGTON CARVER
PROFESSOR JAMES G. WILSON
SECRETARY
TWO REPORTERS
YOUNG MAN

SCENE 1

TIME: *The early 1870's.*

SETTING: *Interior of log house. There is a door up center and a window in left wall. At right is rough fireplace with cooking utensils hanging near it and rough mantel above it. There are pieces of pewter and roll of knitting on mantel. Two wooden beds are against upstage wall, on either side of door, and table is at center. Around table are two or three stools. Spinning wheel and stool stand downstage.*

39

AT RISE: AUNT SUE CARVER, *a middle-aged white woman, sits at spinning wheel, spinning. Door opens, and* GEORGE, *a small black boy of about ten, appears in doorway carrying a basket filled with plants, grasses, and flowers. He wears a wildflower in the buttonhole of his shirt.*

GEORGE *(Excitedly):* Aunt Sue!

AUNT SUE: George, where have you been? Uncle Mose is angry. He's been looking for you all morning.

GEORGE: I—I'm sorry, Aunt Sue. I didn't know I was gone long. I went to the woods.

AUNT SUE: Well, don't come inside with your rubbish.

GEORGE: But it isn't rubbish, Aunt Sue. I've found the most wonderful new bug!

AUNT SUE *(Sarcastically):* Bugs—wonderful. A bug is a bug.

GEORGE: And some kind of grass I've never seen before and a beautiful wildflower. *(Points to buttonhole)* See—I've got it in my buttonhole.

AUNT SUE *(Softening):* The flowers you bring back *are* beautiful. Those wild ones you've planted in the yard— the neighbors all say how lucky I am to have such a fine garden.

GEORGE: But if only I know the names of the flowers and what to call the bugs and what makes the different colors—

AUNT SUE: Questions, questions! Do you never get tired of asking questions? George, you should be going to school.

GEORGE: I have learned some from the speller you gave me.

AUNT SUE: But it isn't enough. You cannot learn the names of your bugs or your flowers from the speller—

you need to learn other things. Now, you'd better take your plants outside. Uncle Mose needs you.

GEORGE: But I wanted to show you what I have in the basket.

AUNT SUE *(Smiling):* All right. *(She puts her work down and gets up.* GEORGE *shuts door and comes downstage toward her.)* You ought to rest a bit after that long, hot walk to the woods, anyway. (GEORGE *takes plant out of basket and holds it up.)*

GEORGE: Look at this, Aunt Sue.

AUNT SUE *(Taking it):* What is this you've dug up so carefully? A weed?

GEORGE *(Taking it away from her):* No—no! It's a plant. It grows, so it must be good for something. I want to know what—

AUNT SUE: Want to know—want to know. I never saw such a child.

GEORGE: I wonder about everything, Aunt Sue. The other day, when I was in the woods, it started to rain, so I sat under a tree and the little ones sat with me.

AUNT SUE *(Puzzled):* Little ones? I suppose you mean the animals.

GEORGE: Yes! A rabbit, two squirrels, and a chipmunk. We all just sat there and waited until the rain stopped. And then there was a bright rainbow, and I started wondering about that. The colors were just like the colors in the flowers. You know, Aunt Sue, all those colors must be in the earth.

AUNT SUE: Why do you say that, George?

GEORGE: Well, the flowers grow right up out of the earth. The colors must come from somewhere.

AUNT SUE *(Affectionately):* If anyone ever finds them, you will.

GEORGE: And we can use those colors, Aunt Sue—look at this! *(He takes a flat stone from basket.)*

AUNT SUE *(As she examines it closely):* You've painted a picture on a stone! Where did you get the paint?

GEORGE: I made it from pikeberries, and I made a little brush from horse hair.

AUNT SUE: Where did you get the idea of painting pictures?

GEORGE: The other day, when Uncle Mose sent me to Farmer Baynham's on an errand, Mrs. Baynham took me in to look at her plants and showed me some pictures hanging on the walls in the parlor.

AUNT SUE *(Smiling):* So you had to try your hand at the same thing.

GEORGE: Well, while I was looking at them, I thought, "I can do that!" *(Matter of factly)* and I did. *(There is a knock on door.)*

AUNT SUE: George, will you put your things outside and see who that is?

GEORGE: Yes, Aunt Sue. *(He opens door for* MARTHA, *who carries package tied with string.)*

GEORGE: Oh, hello.

AUNT SUE *(Crossing to door):* Why, Martha, how nice of you to come by. Come in!

MARTHA *(Entering):* Hello, Mrs. Carver. Mother sent me on an errand.

AUNT SUE: Well, I'm glad she did. *(Leads* MARTHA *downstage)* I don't get to see my neighbors in Diamond Grove half often enough. (GEORGE *sets basket down outside door and comes in again, closing door behind him.)*

MARTHA *(Holding out package):* Mother made you a loaf of fresh corn bread.

AUNT SUE: How nice of her! She makes the best corn

bread I've ever tasted. *(She takes package and slips off string, which drops to floor as she pulls back paper.)* It looks delicious! *(She sets bread on table. GEORGE spies string and darts behind AUNT SUE to pick it up.)*

GEORGE: Aunt Sue, you dropped the string. *(He quickly winds string into little ball.)*

AUNT SUE: So I did. *(To MARTHA)* George is such a thrifty one! Saves everything. By the way, Martha, do you know our boy, George? George, this is Martha from the farm over the hill.

GEORGE: Afternoon, Martha.

MARTHA: Good afternoon, George. You're the one I've really come to see. Mother thought maybe you could do something about our garden. Everyone in town says you have such a way with plants.

AUNT SUE: That he has. I believe he was born with a green thumb. All green things seem to grow under his touch.

MARTHA *(Smiling; to GEORGE)*: I wish you could help us with our roses. We put them in last spring, and they did nicely for a while, but now the leaves are turning brown.

GEORGE: Maybe they don't get enough water or sunshine. I could tell if I saw them. *(Eagerly)* Could I go see them now, Aunt Sue?

AUNT SUE: Of course you may go, George, but not now. Your Uncle Mose will be wanting you to help him outside. Perhaps tomorrow. *(Door opens and UNCLE MOSE, a stern-looking white man, enters.)*

UNCLE MOSE *(Sharply)*: George, where you have been?

AUNT SUE: Mose, we have a caller.

MARTHA: Afternoon, Mr. Carver.

UNCLE MOSE *(Turning)*: Oh, how do you do, Martha?

(Turning back to GEORGE*)* George, didn't I tell you to finish chopping the wood this morning?

GEORGE *(Beginning to stammer):* I—I—I—

UNCLE MOSE *(Impatiently):* Well, answer me!

AUNT SUE *(More gently):* Did he tell you to do that, George?

GEORGE: Yes, Aunt Sue, but I—I forgot.

UNCLE MOSE: *Forgot?* Is that any excuse?

GEORGE: Oh, Aunt Sue, can't you make Uncle Mose understand? When I'm in the woods, I cannot think of anything but the plants, and the time passes so quickly. I didn't know it was so late.

AUNT SUE: He can do the work now, Mose. Go on, George. You'd better hurry.

GEORGE: Yes, Aunt Sue. *(He starts out.)*

UNCLE MOSE: The ax is by the door, and see that you use it this time.

GEORGE: Yes, Uncle Mose. *(He exits.)*

UNCLE MOSE *(To* MARTHA*)*: Susan makes excuses for the boy, and he *is* a good boy in many ways—but he must learn to do his work.

AUNT SUE: He's a big help with the cooking and cleaning, and when I put up preserves—

UNCLE MOSE: But what kind of work is that for a man? He has to learn to plow, so he'll be able to make a living. *(Sighs heavily)* Well, back to work. *(He turns to leave, then stops, turning to* MARTHA.*)* It was good to see you, Martha.

MARTHA: Good to see you, too, Mr. Carver. (UNCLE MOSE *exits and closes door.*)

AUNT SUE: Sit down, Martha.

MARTHA: Thank you. (MARTHA *sits on stool at left of table.* AUNT SUE *sits on stool at right.*)

AUNT SUE: You know, my husband does not mean to be hard on the boy, but he does not always understand George. He's been as good to George as if he were our own son.

MARTHA: Has George always lived with you, Mrs. Carver?

AUNT SUE: Yes. Perhaps you're too young to remember when we had all the trouble in Missouri between those who believed in slavery and those who didn't.

MARTHA: I remember some of it, and I've heard stories.

AUNT SUE: Well, we were always against slavery. My husband brought George's mother here—her name was Mary. *(Sadly, remembering)* She was a fine girl.

MARTHA *(Tentatively):* Did she die?

AUNT SUE: We don't know. *(Sadly)* She was stolen by night raiders, and we never saw her again.

MARTHA: How about George's father?

AUNT SUE: He was a slave on the Grant place—the Baynhams own it now. Mose always wanted big George to come here, too, so Mary and he could be together, but we couldn't afford it. A few months before the raiders took Mary, big George was killed while he was hauling wood.

MARTHA: And you kept the baby.

AUNT SUE: Yes, and his older brother, Jim. But Jim's different. He's always been strong. He can do heavy work, and he helps on other farms, too. George has always been a bit sickly. His voice is still weak, and he stammers sometimes.

MARTHA: But he's such a bright boy!

AUNT SUE *(Nodding):* It is remarkable. Why, it seems he can do anything! (*She rises, goes to mantel and picks up a long strip of knitting in different colors;*

showing it to MARTHA) Look at this. George is knitting it.

MARTHA *(Surprised):* Knitting? *(Examining it)* It's beautiful work.

AUNT SUE: Yes—and I never taught him. He was watching me one day and said, "Aunt Sue, I could do that." Later, he made some needles from turkey feathers and sat down and started this. *(Puts knitting back on mantel)*

MARTHA: He seems to be able to do anything with his hands! How do you account for his knowing so much about plants?

AUNT SUE: No one can account for that. It's just—well, uncanny. And it seems he's always searching to learn more. *(Door opens suddenly, and* GEORGE *runs in, followed by* UNCLE MOSE. GEORGE *carries a branch and is obviously frightened.* UNCLE MOSE *is angry and catches hold of* GEORGE's *shoulder, but* GEORGE *breaks away and runs to* AUNT SUE.)

UNCLE MOSE *(Angrily):* Don't you go whimpering to your aunt. She won't save you this time! *(He grabs* GEORGE *by the arm and pulls him away from* AUNT SUE.)

AUNT SUE: Mose, you're hurting the boy! (MARTHA *looks frightened.)*

UNCLE MOSE: Susan, the boy is to be punished this time—and severely!

GEORGE *(Stammering):* P—p—please, Aunt Sue.

AUNT SUE: What has he done, Mose?

UNCLE MOSE: Instead of chopping the wood as I told him, he took the ax and started chopping at our finest apple tree!

AUNT SUE *(Shocked):* But George wouldn't hurt a tree!

UNCLE MOSE (*Pointing at branch* GEORGE *is holding*): There's your proof—right in his hand. The apple branch he chopped off!

AUNT SUE (*Shocked*): George! There must have been some reason—

UNCLE MOSE (*Loudly*): Reason? You talk of reason?

GEORGE (*Stammering*): Aunt Sue, I—I—tried—to—to—tell him. (*Holds up branch*) S—see?

AUNT SUE: Tell him what, George?

GEORGE: I—I wanted to—to show him, but he—he wouldn't listen.

AUNT SUE: George, wait a minute, child. You're so excited, I can't understand you.

UNCLE MOSE: Susan, you're always making excuses for the boy.

AUNT SUE: Mose, you know George stammers when he's overexcited. He loses his voice. (*Calmly; to* GEORGE) George, try to tell me.

GEORGE (*Holding out branch*): B-bugs, Aunt Sue, b—bugs all over the branch!

AUNT SUE (*Peering at branch*): What? What's that?

GEORGE (*More calmly, speaking more plainly*): Tiny bugs crawling on it, see?

AUNT SUE: So there are. Look, Mose, little bugs. You can hardly see them.

UNCLE MOSE (*Examining branch*): Why, you're right.

GEORGE: I—I tried to tell you, Uncle Mose. (*To* AUNT SUE) I ran to him, Aunt Sue, and I pulled at him, but he wouldn't listen. He kept telling me to chop the wood.

UNCLE MOSE: I couldn't understand him, Susan.

GEORGE: The bugs would spread and kill the tree. I—I had to do something.

MARTHA (*Moving toward* GEORGE *and looking at branch*): Why, I believe these are the same bugs that attacked one of our trees at home, and the tree died!

UNCLE MOSE (*Embarrassed*): I don't know what to say. I've looked at that tree a dozen times, and I didn't see them.

MARTHA: But George did!

AUNT SUE: Oh, Mose, it's just as I've tried to tell you. The boy has some great gift. Small as he is, he sees things we don't see—about plants, about many things.

UNCLE MOSE: I'm beginning to believe you're right, Susan.

AUNT SUE (*Firmly*): And he must go to school so that he can learn.

MARTHA (*To* UNCLE MOSE): There's a school in Neosho, the county seat, where they would take him.

GEORGE (*Eagerly*): Oh, Aunt Sue—Uncle Mose . . . I'd do anything if I could go to school!

UNCLE MOSE: It will be hard for the boy—alone. Neosho is so far away. He couldn't come back here at night to eat and sleep.

GEORGE: I don't care if I have to sleep in a barn or outside or anywhere, Uncle Mose, if only I can go to school.

AUNT SUE: I think you can earn your way, George. You could do odd jobs. (GEORGE *nods enthusiastically.*)

UNCLE MOSE (*Worriedly*): But he is so young, and too small to be on his own.

AUNT SUE (*Firmly*): It is what he must do. (*She puts her hand on* GEORGE's *arm.*) I have a strong feeling that he will keep on learning more and more—that he will do wonderful things—that he will be a great man. (*Curtain*)

*   *   *   *   *

SCENE 2

TIME: *The summer of 1896.*

SETTING: *Classroom at Iowa State College. At center is large desk facing left. Books, papers, file boxes for slides, and a microscope are on desk. At right of desk is a swivel chair; at left of desk are two students' desks and chairs. Above desk hang some botanical charts.*

AT RISE: GEORGE WASHINGTON CARVER, *now in his early thirties, is studying a chart. He has a moustache twisted at the ends. His plain suit of clothes is well worn, and in the buttonhole of his coat he wears a flower. After a moment, he turns and starts toward desk, sees something on floor, and stoops to pick it up. It is a piece of string. He opens desk drawer, takes out a ball of string and winds piece on it, then puts ball back in drawer. He sits down at desk and studies a slide through microscope. He takes slide out, puts it in box and makes a notation on a piece of paper. There is a knock on door.*

CARVER: Come in. *(He puts another slide under microscope, and JAMES G. WILSON, a middle-aged white professor, enters.)*

WILSON: Well, George, I see you're working late, as usual.

CARVER *(Starting to rise):* Oh, Professor Wilson.

WILSON: Don't get up. (CARVER *sits down again.*) You ought to be celebrating tonight, now that you are to receive your master's degree. George Washington Carver—Bachelor of Science, Master of Science.

CARVER: I *am* celebrating, working on my mycological collection. It's never been properly catalogued before.

WILSON *(Picking up a slide and looking at it):* A great collection. How many specimens are there now?

CARVER: Over twenty thousand.

WILSON: George, that's wonderful! (WILSON *pulls up chair and sits opposite* GEORGE.) You've traveled a long, hard road, George.

CARVER: It has been long, sir, but I don't know about hard.

WILSON *(Shaking his head):* I don't know how you did it. Going to school in so many different places, traveling from town to town, working at odd jobs—with no family of your own.

CARVER: But in a way I did have families, sir, many families. People were always so kind. The Carvers treated me as their own son, and in Neosho Aunt Mariah Watkins took me in. Then there were the Seymours and the Milhollands, and last but not least, all of you here at Ames.

WILSON *(Smiling):* Ames was fortunate indeed that you came here. Iowa State College has never had a more brilliant student, and your work here these last two years on the faculty as an assistant botanist has been outstanding.

CARVER: I couldn't have done it without your help.

WILSON: It seems to me you've always helped yourself most of all. The way you've worked—waiting on tables, doing laundry, anything you could put your hands to.

CARVER: But I enjoy working with my hands.

WILSON: And a good thing, since you have to earn your own way.

CARVER: But think of all you've done for me, Professor Wilson—buying the ticket for me to go to that art exhibit, seeing that my paintings got hung—

WILSON: Well, that was certainly worthwhile. Weren't

your paintings chosen to hang in the World's Colum-
bian Exposition?

CARVER *(Musing):* Ah, my paintings. You know, ever
since I was a boy I've thought perhaps I'd like to be a
great artist and go to Paris to study. There's always
been a conflict between that and my work with plants,
but there isn't time for everything.

WILSON: Have you given up the idea of studying art?

CARVER: Yes, sir. I feel I can be of more service to others
in agriculture.

WILSON: That's like you, George, to think of what you
can do for others. You have so many talents, but
there's no one who can touch you in the field of agriculture. Your work with grafting, cross-breeding and
hybridization has been recognized by authorities all
over the country. And now the final step, George.
(After a pause) You're to be given a full professorship
here at Ames.

CARVER *(Overwhelmed):* It's a honor, sir, but I'm afraid
I can't accept.

WILSON *(Astonished):* Why not?

CARVER: You knew that Booker T. Washington of
Tuskegee Institute in Alabama had written, asking me
to be in charge of their agriculture department.

WILSON: Yes, but I didn't know you were considering it
seriously.

CARVER: I feel I must go.

WILSON: But Tuskegee offered you only fifteen hundred
dollars a year. That's not a large salary, George.

CARVER: No, but money is not important to me. My
needs are few.

WILSON *(Laughing a little):* True. No one could ever
accuse you of wasting your money. But George, have

you thought over what it will mean to you? Here we have all the most modern equipment—you can go on with your experiments.

CARVER: I expect to continue with my experiments at Tuskegee.

WILSON: But they have so little laboratory equipment!

CARVER: I know that, and Mr. Washington realizes it, too.

WILSON: Then how can you do as much there?

CARVER (*Fervently*): There must be a way! Alabama has soil, sunshine, and rain—it will be a challenge for me. I'm certain that land can produce a living for all its people!

WILSON (*Shaking his head*): Well, if there is anything in that land, you're the man to find it! (*Upset*) But I just can't think of your leaving Ames. I always thought your future should be here.

CARVER: Perhaps if you read Mr. Washington's letter, you'd understand, Professor Wilson. (*He takes a letter from his coat pocket and hands it to* WILSON.)

WILSON (*Scanning the letter*): "Hm—m . . . (*Reads*) "The students, barefoot, come for miles over bad roads. They are thin and in rags. You would not understand such poverty." (WILSON *looks up at* CARVER *and smiles.*) Mr. Washington evidently doesn't know much about your background, George.

CARVER: No, I guess he doesn't.

WILSON (*Reading*): "I cannot offer you money, position or fame. I offer you in their place work—hard, hard work—the task of bringing a people from degradation, poverty, and waste to full manhood." (WILSON *looks at* CARVER *in silence for a moment.*) George, you have made the only decision that you could make. This is something bigger than personal ambition.

CARVER (*Smiling*): I'm glad you understand.

WILSON: All of us who know you best will understand. We here at Ames will miss you and your work, but we must recognize what you must do.

CARVER: Thank you, Professor Wilson. It will make it easier for me knowing my friends approve the step I'm taking. (WILSON *shakes his hand.*)

WILSON: Our blessings go with you, and I know all your efforts will be crowned with success. (*Curtain*)

* * * * *

SCENE 3

TIME: *1937.*

SETTING: *Carver's study at Tuskegee. Large window with many plants in window box is center. Books line walls on either side of window. On side walls hang many pictures and embroideries. Door is down. left; upstage from door is glass case containing geological collection. Large, old desk, piled high with papers and books, is against right wall; there is a microscope on desk and a push button on side of desk. In front of desk is a chair; next to desk is a wastebasket. Large table piled with miscellaneous collection of geological specimens and magnifying glass is center. There are chairs about the room, and every corner is crammed with plants, pieces of embroidery, specimens, etc.*

AT RISE: CARVER *is working on plant. His hair and moustache are white, and his shoulders are bent. His clothes look well-worn; he wears a flower in the buttonhole of his lapel. He lifts plant from table and examines it; picking up magnifying glass, he exam-*

ines plant more closely. The door opens left and black SECRETARY *enters. She carries sheet of paper in one hand and bundle of mail tied with a piece of string in the other.*

SECRETARY: Good morning, Dr. Carver.

CARVER: Good morning.

SECRETARY: Here's the mail—over a hundred letters again today.

CARVER: My, my, think of that. It always surprises me how many people find time to write. *(Chuckling)* They always start by saying how busy they know I am and then they go on for pages.

SECRETARY: And it's such work for you, Doctor, to go through them all. I could take care of some of it for you.

CARVER: Yes, I daresay you could, but the truth is I like reading them. Besides, I've been answering letters like this for so many years that when they ask questions about their soil or water or crops, I know just what they mean.

SECRETARY: Yes, I suppose you are the only one who can do it, but there are so many other things—*(She consults the sheet of paper.)* You've a very busy day ahead.

CARVER: Is that so? *(He takes another plant from table and looks at it admiringly.)* You know, I had a very successful walk this morning—seventeen different varieties—now, look at this, did you ever see a more beautiful specimen?

SECRETARY *(Smiling):* It's a fine specimen, Doctor, but your list of appointments—*(She holds out list.)*

CARVER: *(Putting down plant):* Oh, very well. What do we have today? *(He walks over to desk and sits down facing her, folding his hands in a resigned manner.)*

SECRETARY *(Consulting sheet):* Well, at eleven o'clock,

you're to meet with that committee from Washington—something about dehydration.

CARVER: Ah, yes, I've been preaching dehydration for thirty years, and now the bigwigs are really interested. You'd think it was the first time they had ever heard of it.

SECRETARY: And then that Horticultural Society is visiting here today. You promised to speak to them at one o'clock.

CARVER: So I did.

SECRETARY *(Consulting list again):* There's a man from California who wants to know something about the paints you've made from our Alabama clay.

CARVER: Oh, yes, he owns a large paint company, and he's going to offer me a lot of money to go to work for him.

SECRETARY *(Anxiously):* Doctor, we're not going to lose you, are we?

CARVER *(Smiling):* No, you're not. I'm not in the business of making money. I wouldn't know what to do with it if I made it by the bushel. Well, is that all?

SECRETARY: No—right now there are two reporters waiting to interview you. That's the first thing.

CARVER *(Shaking his head):* Oh, my, I don't like talking to reporters.

SECRETARY: I know, but they say their paper's been trying to get a story for a long time about the—*(She stops and smiles.)* the Wizard of Tuskegee.

CARVER *(Smiling, too, but shaking his head):* Wizard of Tuskegee? Well, I'll set them right on that. Show them in.

SECRETARY: Yes, Doctor. *(She unties bundle of letters, drops string in wastebasket, and puts bundle on desk.)* Here's your mail. *(She turns and exits.* CARVER *reaches into wastebasket and pulls out string. He opens desk drawer, takes out ball of string, and carefully winds piece around. He puts ball back into drawer as* SECRETARY *enters, followed by two white* REPORTERS, *who carry notebooks and pencils.)*

SECRETARY: Dr. Carver, these are the gentlemen from the *Courier.*

REPORTERS: Good morning, Doctor.

CARVER: Good morning, gentlemen. Won't you sit down? *(He motions to chairs near table.* REPORTERS *sit.* SECRETARY *exits left.)*

CARVER: Well, now that you've cornered me in my lair, what can I do for you?

1ST REPORTER: Well, sir, there have been so many things printed about what you've done that we thought we'd like to get the story of your life.

CARVER *(Humorously):* Dear me, that's a large order. There are so many ramifications. Perhaps if you would just ask me questions . . .

2ND REPORTER: Of course, we know about all the honors you've received—the degrees, the Springarn Medal—

1ST REPORTER: And all the fine offers you've had. Didn't Edison want you to work for him once? *(During following dialogue,* REPORTERS *periodically take notes.)*

CARVER: Yes, he did.

1ST REPORTER: Would you care to quote the salary he offered?

CARVER *(Hesitating):* No. No, I wouldn't, but if it's of great interest to you, it was six figures.

1ST REPORTER *(Impressed):* A hundred thousand dollars is a lot of money, sir. What made you turn it down?

CARVER: Well, you see, I have no real use for that kind of money. I wanted to stay on here at Tuskegee—besides, I'd promised Booker T. Washington that I would.

2ND REPORTER: You were very close to Mr. Washington, weren't you?

CARVER: Yes, we worked together for many years. We watched Tuskegee grow from a poor, struggling school to the fine institution it is today.

1ST REPORTER: Are you still teaching, Dr. Carver?

CARVER: No. Mr. Washington released me from my teaching duties before he died, so that I could spend all my time on research. But I still keep my eye on the students. You see, I'm still a student myself. Every day I learn something—why, you take these specimens I picked up this morning—*(He rises and goes to table, stopping abruptly)* Oh, dear—

2ND REPORTER: Is something wrong, sir?

CARVER: No—but you'll have to excuse me for a moment. I've forgotten something. *(He picks up a plant, goes to desk, taking specimen with him. He scribbles something on a scrap of paper.)* You see, I discovered a very rare species of fungi this morning—I must send it to the United States Department of Agriculture right away. *(He presses button at side of desk.)*

2ND REPORTER: A new species? *(With pencil poised)* What is it?

CARVER *(Dryly; rattling it off):* Why, it's a specimen of Pandanus javanicus variegatus attacked by Diplodia natalansis.

2ND REPORTER: Oh, I see. (SECRETARY *enters.*)

SECRETARY: Yes, Dr. Carver?

CARVER: Will you take this to the laboratory? Ask Mr. Curtis to have it prepared and sent off at once. *(He hands her note and specimen.)*

SECRETARY: Yes, sir. *(She exits left.)*

CARVER: Please excuse the interruption, gentlemen. I noticed you eyeing my cluttered desk. *(Gestures)* It's rather dreadful—I once had an assistant who classified this conglomeration as orderly disorder.

2ND REPORTER *(Laughing):* Well, it does look a little confusing.

CARVER: But I really can find things, you know. *(He delves into pile of papers and comes up triumphantly with a few small envelopes.)* Here, for instance, are some packets of flower seeds that have to go off today.

2ND REPORTER: Are you sending them to some horticultural society?

CARVER: No, just to friends. *(As he holds up packet)* These go to a lady six miles from here, and these to a gentleman in Arizona, and these to a professor in Germany.

1ST REPORTER *(Pointing to paintings on wall):* These paintings are your own work, aren't they, Dr. Carver? I've heard you're an artist. *(Rises to examine them more closely)*

CARVER: Yes, but I haven't had much time to spend on my painting since coming to Tuskegee. I did most of these to show the students what could be done with the colors in Alabama clay.

1ST REPORTER: Pigments from clay? *(Stopping before a still life)* This is a fine study.

CARVER: Ah, yes. That illustrates a new techinique. I did it with my fingertips instead of a brush.

1ST REPORTER *(Impressed):* Amazing. *(Pointing to one of the embroideries on wall)* I see you have some beautiful samples of embroidery—are they of some particular interest?

CARVER: Oh, not really. I make them from time to time for relaxation.

1ST REPORTER (*Surprised*): *You* make them?

CARVER: Yes, I learned to do it when I was a boy. (2ND REPORTER *rises, looks into case up left.*)

2ND REPORTER: What's in the case, Dr. Carver? It looks like a diamond!

CARVER (*Crossing to join* 2ND REPORTER): It is. There are many varieties of native quartz, and one of them happens to be a diamond.

1ST REPORTER (*As he looks at diamond*): Isn't that worth a lot of money?

CARVER: Oh, I expect it is. How I came by it is rather amusing. You see, I'd helped a gentleman who manufactures peanut butter. He'd had trouble with the oil rising to the top, and I showed him how to avoid that. He was so grateful he asked me what I wanted. I told him I'd like a diamond, so he sent it to me, mounted in a beautiful ring.

2ND REPORTER (*Amused*): He thought you wanted to wear it.

CARVER: Of course, and I guess he was a little taken aback when he found I'd put it in my geological collection.

1ST REPORTER (*Laughing*): No wonder. (*All sit.*)

2ND REPORTER: Peanuts are one of your specialties, aren't they, Doctor?

CARVER: Gentlemen, you can make most anything from the peanut. When I first started working on peanuts, I was amazed.

2ND REPORTER: How many products have you developed?

CARVER: Over three hundred, including milk, cream,

coffee, paper, stains, plastics—

1ST REPORTER: Plastics? That's becoming an important industry now, isn't it?

CARVER: Yes, it is, but twenty years ago we were making what they call plastics today from peanuts, sweet potatoes, and many other plants right here at Tuskegee.

2ND REPORTER: I didn't realize that.

CARVER: I find that with most scientific developments there is a lapse of about twenty years between the laboratory work and actually putting the knowledge to use. (SECRETARY *enters left.*)

SECRETARY: Excuse me, Dr. Carver—

CARVER: Yes?

SECRETARY: I don't like to bother you, but there's a young man here who insists on seeing you. He says it will only take a minute.

CARVER: Very well. I'm sure these gentlemen won't mind.

1ST REPORTER: Of course not. (SECRETARY *starts for door, then turns back.*)

SECRETARY: Oh, and there's another thing. The treasurer's office called about your salary checks that are still uncashed. The auditors are coming soon, and they'd like you to cash your checks so they can balance the books.

CARVER: Dear me, we had the same trouble last year, didn't we?

SECRETARY *(Shaking her head, gently reprimanding him):* Yes, we did, Dr. Carver.

CARVER: I know they're all here somewhere. In fact, I saw one just this morning. *(He dives into pile of papers on desk and brings up a check.)* You see? A nice, fresh one—it's only six months old!

SECRETARY *(Shaking her head; smiling):* I'll send the young man in. *(She exits.)*

CARVER: I suppose I should try to be more careful, but there's not much sense cashing these checks unless I need the money, and I can't spend fifteen hundred dollars a year.

2ND REPORTER *(Surprised):* Fifteen hundred! You mean that's your salary here?

CARVER: Why, yes. It's the amount Mr. Washington offered me when I came here in 1896, and I've been getting it ever since.

1ST REPORTER: It's not very much.

CARVER *(Laughing):* Well, I guess if they thought I was worth more they'd pay me more. *(He pauses; then laughing)* I'm only making a joke, gentlemen. They've tried to increase my salary, but, well, you see, I don't need what I have. It seems to me people place an exaggerated importance on money. *(He stops, seeing* YOUNG MAN, *black, standing in doorway.)* Oh, come in. I'm delighted to see you. (CARVER *crosses to greet* YOUNG MAN, *shakes his hand. Then with one hand on his shoulder, he draws* YOUNG MAN *down center.)*

YOUNG MAN: Thank you, Professor Carver. I'm sorry to interrupt like this, but I didn't have much time.

CARVER: Not much time? Well, that's good. That shows you're busy.

YOUNG MAN: Yes sir, I am, but the last time I saw you, you told me to come back and report—about the dollar you gave me.

CARVER: So I did. Well, what have you done with it?

YOUNG MAN: Well, I bought a hen for fifty cents and a setting of eggs for fifteen—the rest I used for feed.

CARVER *(Nodding his head):* Yes . . .

YOUNG MAN: Well, the eggs hatched out all right, and

then *(Excitedly)* some more and then some more—
well, now, sir, I've got seventy-five hens bringing in
money. You wouldn't believe it, Professor Carver, but
now I've saved up fifty-one dollars, and I'm going to
pay it down on a lot.

CARVER: Fine. You've got a start on a place of your own.
That's what I like to see.

YOUNG MAN: I have to go now. There's a bus leaving in a
few minutes.

CARVER: Let me know when you have two hundred
chickens! Goodbye. (YOUNG MAN *exits.* CARVER *turns
back to* REPORTERS.)

1ST REPORTER: That young man seems to be doing all
right.

CARVER: Of course he is! Now, that's what I call a proper
expenditure of money. By adding a little common
sense and a lot of hard work to that dollar, he's made
something worthwhile out of it.

2ND REPORTER: He certainly didn't waste any of it.

CARVER: No waste. That's the secret. There need never
be waste. It's what we have been teaching here ever
since this school began. And by doing just that, we
have prospered.

1ST REPORTER: It's wonderful.

CARVER: Everything has a purpose—even a weed.

2ND REPORTER: Then why don't we make use of the
weeds?

CARVER: We will. In fact, we have, here at Tuskegee. A
weed is simply a plant growing where we don't want it
to grow. If we cultivate it properly, it can be used. And
it's the same with all other forms of waste. Corn
stalks, peanut shells, wood shavings—

1ST REPORTER: You've made marble from wood shavings, haven't you, Doctor?

CARVER: Yes, and that's only one thing. Some day all the

waste products of agriculture will be used in industry. There is untold wealth lying all about us, if we will but look for it—a fourth kingdom, I like to call it. (SECRE-TARY *enters left.)*

SECRETARY: Dr. Carver, I'm sorry for all these interruptions, but there are two little boys outside with a very sick dog.

CARVER: A dog?

SECRETARY: Yes. They have walked miles lugging the poor animal, and they say if the "Professor" will just look at him, he'll be all right.

CARVER *(Laughing):* I'm sorry, gentlemen. You'll have to excuse me again. *(They smile as he crosses left and follows* SECRETARY *out.)*

1ST REPORTER *(Shaking his head):* What a man!

2ND REPORTER: He's amazing—doing the finest creative research in the country, and he takes time to look at a sick dog!

1ST REPORTER *(Rising and walking about; enthusiastically):* Well, we've got a story. Do you see it the way I do? It's not so much the honors he's received or the big things he's done—it's just one human being working for the good of all the others.

2ND REPORTER: That's it exactly. Why, the whole story of his life is one of service to others. He lives it every day.

1ST REPORTER: And that's what we want to write about. He hasn't given us any dates, but we can easily look them up in *Who's Who.*

2ND REPORTER *(Rising):* Sure, there's a copy right on the shelves here. I wonder what it says about him. *(He takes copy of* Who's Who in America *from shelf and thumbs through it.)* Here it is! *(Reads)* "Carver, George Washington—born a slave, 1864—worked way through high school, Minneapolis, Kansas, and later through college—B.S. Agriculture, Iowa State College, 1894—M.S. Agriculture, 1896. Member of Royal Society of Arts, London—"*(He stops, looks up.)* Born a slave—made a member of the Royal Society of Arts in London. I'll bet he's the only one who ever bridged that gap! *(He shuts book and puts it back on shelf. CARVER re-enters, smiling.)*

1ST REPORTER: Well, Doctor? How's the dog?

CARVER: A slight case of distemper, but he'll live. In fact, we're going to keep him right here for a few days, until he recovers.

1ST REPORTER: Dr. Carver, I think we've taken up enough of your time.

CARVER: Well, I—I haven't told you very much, I'm afraid.

2ND REPORTER: Oh, we have our story all right. Thanks so much, Doctor, for giving us the interview.

CARVER: You're entirely welcome. *(They shake hands; REPORTERS start to exit left.)*

1ST REPORTER *(Turning):* Oh, by the way, Dr. Carver, is there any particular statement you'd like to make?

CARVER *(Smiling):* There is one thing, gentlemen. Please don't refer to me as a wizard. I'm not one, you know.

1ST REPORTER: Very well, sir. We won't. We'll just tell the truth. We'll say that you're a truly great man. *(They exit. CARVER walks toward stage center, shaking his head.)*

CARVER: Great man—humph! Now, let me see—where was I? Oh, yes. *(He walks to table, takes a plant from basket, picks up magnifying glass, examines plant as curtain falls.)*

THE END

PRODUCTION NOTES

GEORGE WASHINGTON CARVER

Characters: 7 male; 3 female.

Playing Time: 40 minutes.

Costumes: All characters wear clothes appropriate to periods represented. Carver's clothes are a bit shabby, and he always wears flower in buttonhole.

Properties: Scene 1: Basket filled with plants, grasses, flat stone; package tied with string containing loaf of bread; branch. Scene 3: Sheet of paper; bundle of mail tied with string; notebooks and pencils.

Setting: Scene 1: Interior of log house. There is a door up center and a window in left wall. At right is a rough fireplace with cooking utensils hanging near it and a rough mantel above it. There are pieces of pewter and a roll of knitting on mantel. There are two wooden beds against upstage wall on either side of door and a table at center. Around table are two or three stools. A spinning wheel and stool stand downstage. Scene 2: Classroom at Iowa State College. At center is a large desk facing left. Books, papers, file boxes for slides, and a microscope are on desk. At right of desk is swivel chair; at left of desk are two students' desks and chairs. Above desk hang botanical charts. There is a piece of string on floor and a ball of string in desk drawer. Scene 3: Carver's study at Tuskegee. Large window with many plants in window box is center. Books line walls on either side of window. On side walls hang many pictures and embroideries. Door is downstage left; upstage from door is glass case containing geological collection. Large, old desk, piled high with papers and books, is against right wall; there is a microscope on desk and a push button on side of desk. In front of desk is a chair and down from desk is a wastebasket. Large table piled with miscellaneous collection of geological specimens and magnifying glass is center. There are chairs about the room, and every corner is crammed with plants, pieces of embroidery, specimens, etc.

Lighting and Sound: No special effects.

John Henry

by Barbara Winther

Characters

BALLAD SINGER
POLLY ANNE
LITTLE BILL
JOHN HENRY
SAM, *the salesman*
CAPTAIN TOMMY
TWO MEN
TWO WOMEN
PEOPLE, *extras*

AUTHOR'S NOTE

The Swannanoa tunnel, built in West Virginia in the 1880's, was the longest and most difficult tunnel ever cut through a mountain. It was on this tunnel that John Henry, a legendary black man, was supposed to have worked. John became the hero of the southern working men, especially railroad builders, who sang about his strength and his courage as they worked. The ballad, with its many verses telling the exploits of John Henry, is the basis for this play.

SCENE 1

BEFORE RISE: BALLAD SINGER, *carrying guitar, enters in front of curtain, playing and singing to tune of folk song "John Henry," with interjections from* PEOPLE *offstage.*

SINGER: John Henry was a black man hero,

PEOPLE: Uh-huh!

SINGER: Born in West Virginia, they say.

PEOPLE: That's right!

SINGER: He could split a boulder with a hammer,

PEOPLE: Hallelujah!

SINGER: And he grew to a man in one day.

PEOPLE: Praise the Lord.

SINGER: And he grew to a man in one day. *(Speaking, as* PEOPLE *hum in background)* Then John Henry took his twenty-pound hammer, said goodbye to his mammy and pappy and started off across the United States. He was hunting for something. He didn't know what—happiness, maybe, or peace in his soul. All over the country he worked, using his hammer to lay tracks for the railroads. *(Sound of train whistle is heard, followed by rhythmic sound of steel hitting steel, continuing until curtain opens.* SINGER *resumes singing, as before, and* PEOPLE *sing from offstage.)* John Henry had a little woman.

PEOPLE: Uh-huh!

SINGER: Polly Anne was her name.

PEOPLE: That's right!

SINGER: And he worked on the Big Bend Tunnel.

PEOPLE: Oh, yeah!

SINGER: Where his courage and strength brought him fame.

PEOPLE: Hallelujah. (SINGER *starts to exit.)*

SINGER: Where his courage and strength brought him fame. *(Exits. Curtain opens.)*

* * * * *

TIME: *Late afternoon, 1880.*

SETTING: *A country hillside in the southern United States. There is a backdrop painting of hills and forest, with a winding railroad track going through a tunnel, which gives the appearance of leading off right. At center are two tree stumps used as seats.*

AT RISE: POLLY ANNE *enters left and crosses right where she looks off, squinting.* LITTLE BILL *wearily enters right, carrying jacket over shoulder. He tips his cap as he approaches her.*

BILL: Afternoon, Polly Anne.

POLLY: Afternoon, Little Bill. Is John Henry on his way home?

BILL: Your husband is coming up the hill. *(Sits on stump and wipes forehead with bandana)* Whew! I'm worn out. Glad this work day is over.

POLLY *(Wagging her finger, playfully):* Little Bill, all you do is hold the drills while John pounds them into the ground. He does the work while you just watch.

BILL: But John works twice as hard as anyone else, so I have to hold twice as many drills and watch twice as much happen. *(She laughs.* JOHN *enters, carrying hammer.)*

JOHN: Hi, Polly Anne. What's for supper?

POLLY: Three kettles of black-eyed peas, two roast pigs, five possums, a mountain of sweet potatoes, a couple of hills of turnip greens, two hundred biscuits, and five kegs of honey.

JOHN: Sounds mighty good, but I'm powerfully hungry. I doubt that'll be enough to carry me until breakfast.

POLLY *(Shaking head; good-naturedly):* John Henry, your stomach is a bottomless pit. Dinner time is in five minutes—and you'd better bring a shovel. *(Grins and exits)*

JOHN: You know, Little Bill *(Placing foot on other stump and resting elbow on knee),* for the first time in my life I am a contented man. I like living here and working on the railroad for Captain Tommy.

BILL: Captain's a fair man, as bosses go.

JOHN *(Nodding):* That's the truth. *(Crossing right)* See you in the morning, Bill.

BILL: Sure enough, John. (JOHN *exits.* BILL *rises, rubbing shoulder muscles.* SAM *enters left.)*

SAM: Hey, there—you.

BILL: What is it, stranger?

SAM: I'm looking for a man called Captain Tommy.

BILL: You'll find him at the bottom of the hill. *(Points right)*

SAM: Good. *(Hooking thumbs in suspenders, swaggering)* I suspect you'll be seeing a lot of me around here. I've invented something that will change the lives of everyone who works on the railroad.

BILL: What's that?

SAM: Wouldn't do to tell my secret to you. *(Salutes cockily)* Wait until tomorrow. *(Exits right)*

BILL: I don't like the looks of that fellow. I have a feeling something bad is about to happen. *(Train whistle blows as curtain closes.)*

* * * * *

SCENE 2

BEFORE RISE: CAPTAIN TOMMY, *holding paper, with pencil behind ear, enters in front of curtain and*

stands center, reading silently as lights go up. SAM
enters left.

SAM: Are you Captain Tommy?

CAPTAIN: I am.

SAM: Permit me to introduce myself. I am Sam, superior
salesman and owner of Johnson's Steam Drill Company.

CAPTAIN: I'm not buying any newfangled gadgets.
(Starts to write on paper)

SAM: Wait a bit, Captain. Suppose I tell you I've invented a machine that can drive more holes than
twenty men, without resting.

CAPTAIN *(Not looking up):* I'd say you were crazier than
a bedbug and ought to soak your head in a bucket of
water.

SAM *(Crossing arms):* I have this machine here, sir, and
I am willing to show you how fantastic it is.

CAPTAIN *(Slowly looking up):* Well, I suppose I could
take a look at your invention. *(Narrowing eyes)* How
do I know it can do what you claim?

SAM: By testing it. *(Coming closer)* Who is your strong-
est working man?

CAPTAIN: John Henry, without a doubt. *(Tucks pencil
behind ear)*

SAM: I've heard of him.

CAPTAIN: The finest steel-driving man in the country.

SAM: Captain, I propose a race between my steam drill
and your worker, John Henry.

CAPTAIN: How long a race?

SAM: Nine hours.

CAPTAIN: What? You can't expect a man to drive steel
for nine hours.

SAM: Of course not. I expect to show you that my machine will still be working long after John Henry quits.

CAPTAIN: Hm-m-m. I don't know. I'll have to ask John. *(Musing)* Of course, he's never turned his back on a challenge.

SAM *(Extending hand):* Agreed, then?

CAPTAIN: If John wants to do it, it's agreeable with me. *(Clasping* SAM's *hand)* If your steam drill wins, then I'll buy it. If your steam drill loses—

SAM: Yes?

CAPTAIN: Then you have to pay me five hundred dollars.

SAM *(Smiling):* Captain, you drive a hard bargain—but I can't possibly lose, so I accept your terms. *(They shake hands.)* My steam drill will be ready to go in the morning. *(Exits left.* CAPTAIN *starts to write.)*

CAPTAIN: City slickers think their machines have all the answers. *(Looking after* SAM) Who knows? Maybe they do. *(Blackout.* CAPTAIN *exits. Spotlight comes up on* SINGER, *who enters with guitar and plays and sings as before.* PEOPLE *sing from offstage.)*

SINGER: Well, the Captain said to John Henry,
Shall we bring that steam drill around?
Will you race nine hours out on the job,
Driving steel on into the ground?

PEOPLE: Hallelujah.

SINGER: Driving steel on into the ground?

PEOPLE: Then John Henry said to his captain,

SINGER: Well, a man ain't nothing but a man,
But before I let that steam drill beat me down,

PEOPLE: I'll die with a hammer in my hand.

SINGER: Praise the Lord!

PEOPLE: I'll die with a hammer in my hand. *(Spotlight goes out.* SINGER *exits. Curtain opens. Lights come up.)*

*　　*　　*　　*　　*

SCENE 3

TIME: *Late morning, the next day.*
SETTING: *Same as Scene 1.*
AT RISE: *Stage is empty.* JOHN, *carrying hammer,* BILL *and* POLLY *enter left.*

JOHN: Little Bill, will you hold the drills for me in the race?

BILL: I've been doing that for you ever since you came here, John. I won't desert you now.

POLLY: How can I help, John?

JOHN: By bringing me water. I imagine I'll be feeling pretty thirsty as I work.

POLLY: All right. *(Touching* JOHN's *shoulder)* Are you certain you want to enter this race? (JOHN *nods.*) Everyone knows you're the greatest steel-driving man that ever lived. You don't have to prove it. But, John, if a machine breaks down, it can be repaired so it can go on working forever. *(Gently)* But *you* can't go on working forever.

JOHN: No, but I can show how a man can strive for what he cares about. Working on this railroad has been the happiest time of my life. I'm not going to sit back and let a machine take that work away from me, or from others who feel the same way I do about the railroad.

BILL *(To* POLLY): We have to let him do it, Polly Anne. *(Exits right)*

POLLY: I know, Little Bill. I'm just frightened for him. Worried and frightened. *(Exits right, followed by* BILL. CAPTAIN *and* PEOPLE *enter left, humming to tune of "John Henry," as they take places to watch the race. Some point and peer off right, nodding and gesturing to each other. Others may lay blanket on ground, for a picnic.* TWO WOMEN *with open parasols and fancy dresses are escorted by* TWO MEN *to tree stumps, where they sit. By the time the song is hummed through once, all have found places on stage.)*

CAPTAIN *(Shouting off):* On your mark, get set *(Pause),* go. *(Blast of train whistle and then sound of steel hitting steel and chugging of steam engine continue until race is over. Crowd cheers.)*

1ST MAN: Look at John Henry go with that hammer!

2ND MAN: But the steam drill's going just as fast.

1ST WOMAN: And this is a nine-hour race.

2ND WOMAN: John will wear himself out.

1ST WOMAN: I don't see how he can keep up this pace.

1ST MAN: You can bet he'll use every ounce of strength he's got.

2ND MAN: He can't beat a machine.

1ST MAN: Maybe not, but he's got the courage to try.

PEOPLE *(Cheering; ad lib):* Come on, John Henry. You can do it! *(Etc.)*

2ND WOMAN: We're rooting for you.

PEOPLE *(Chanting):* John Henry, John Henry, John Henry . . . *(Chanting fades as lights dim. Spotlight comes up on* SINGER *as he re-enters, playing and singing as before.)*

SINGER: Sunshine was hot and burning,
Wasn't a breeze at all,
Sweat ran down like water down a hill,
That day John Henry let his hammer fall,
Lord! Lord!
That day John Henry let his hammer fall.
(Spotlight goes out. SINGER *exits.* POLLY *enters and stands at right with* CAPTAIN, *so that they can speak to* JOHN, *who is just offstage right.* PEOPLE *begin chanting softly again, as lights go up gradually.)*

PEOPLE *(Chanting):* John Henry, John Henry. . . .
(Continuing softly during the following conversation)

CAPTAIN: John, you've been hammering over eight hours
now. You have to stop. The rock's getting harder and
harder.

POLLY: Please, John, stop now. You're suffering too
much.

JOHN *(Breathlessly, from offstage):* I'm tired. But I
won't give up.

PEOPLE *(Chanting louder):* John Henry, John
Henry . . .

CAPTAIN *(Worriedly):* John, you don't look well. It's the
ninth hour.

POLLY: You've done more than any man could do. Quit
now before it's too late.

JOHN *(Groaning):* No! I'll never quit!

PEOPLE *(Chanting loudly):* John Henry, John
Henry. . . . *(Sound of train whistle is heard. Sounds
of steel striking steel and chugging of steam engine
stop, as does the chanting.)*

CAPTAIN: The race is over. The steam drill drove nine
feet into the mountain. John Henry drove *(Pauses)*
fifteen feet. John Henry wins. (PEOPLE *cheer as* JOHN,
hammer in hand, staggers in, followed by BILL. *CAP-
TAIN helps them over to tree stumps;* POLLY *follows,
looking worried. Seeing* JOHN's *condition,* PEOPLE
quiet down, whispering nervously among themselves.
JOHN *sinks down on one stump.* BILL *sits on other,
wearily holding head in hands.* CAPTAIN *pats* JOHN *on
back.)* John, you've won the biggest race of your life.
We're all mighty proud of you.

SAM: I never thought a man could do it. He beat my
steam drill fair and square. *(Counting out money from*

pocket) Captain, here is the five hundred dollars you won from me.

CAPTAIN *(Taking it):* This is your money, John. *(Holds it out to him)* You're the one who earned it. *(JOHN smiles faintly and shakes his head, then looks at exhausted BILL, reaching out to pat his back but not able to reach it. JOHN stands, shakily, reaches out for POLLY, takes a step and collapses. Men gasp, ladies scream, and children run crying to parents. POLLY kneels beside him.)*

POLLY *(Tearfully):* John, why wouldn't you listen to us? *(Touching hammer)* You just kept on hammering *(Voice faltering)* and hammering and—*(BILL rises and helps her to her feet.)*

BILL *(Comforting her):* Polly Anne, a man has to do what he feels is right. *(She nods and wipes away tears.)*

POLLY: Yes, I know. He was doing that.

CAPTAIN: John Henry, as long as there are people like you, there will never be a machine to take the place of a human spirit. *(Looks at money and then at others, helplessly)* I can't keep this money. Polly, you take it. *(She shakes her head and looks away.)* Well, Sam, I guess you'll just have to take it back. *(Hands it to him)* None of us would feel right having it. (SAM *looks at money, then at JOHN, and shakes head. He exits with bowed head. Everyone freezes as lights dim. Spotlight goes up on SINGER, who enters, playing and singing as before. PEOPLE, including POLLY, BILL and CAPTAIN, join in song.)*

SINGER: Go and tell the story of John Henry,
Born with a hammer that could sing.

PEOPLE: And on hot summer days in the south they say

You can hear his hammer ring.
Lord! Lord!
You can hear his hammer ring.
(*Loud sound of steel striking steel is heard, then fades out as lights go out and curtain closes.*)

THE END

PRODUCTION NOTES

JOHN HENRY

Characters: 6 male; 3 female; 1 male or female for Ballad Singer (preferably plays guitar); and as many as desired for People (at least 4).

Playing Time: 20 minutes.

Costumes: Typical costume of mid-1800's in the South. Bill and John wear work clothes. Bill also wears cap, bandana around neck, and carries jacket in Scene 1. Polly Anne wears long print dress with apron; she removes apron in Scene 2. Captain Tommy wears vest and visor hat. Sam, a flashy pair of pants with suspenders, and straw hat. Two Women wear fancy long dresses, hats, and carry parasols; Two Men wear suits, carry walking sticks.

Properties: Sledge hammer; pencil and paper; blanket; picnic basket; play money.

Setting: Backdrop painting of countryside in southern United States, with train tracks curving across and appearing to lead off right. At center, two tree stumps can be created from stools covered with brown paper.

Lighting: Spotlight and dimming of lights as indicated in text.

Sound: Train whistle blast; hammer striking steel; chugging steam drill, as indicated in text. Offstage voices may be amplified, if desired.

Harriet Tubman—The Second Moses

by Aileen Fisher

Characters

HARRIET TUBMAN
THREE GIRLS
THREE BOYS
CHORUS *(any number)*

1ST GIRL: When Harriet Tubman
Was six years old
Her childhood was over.
Up till then
She had a carefree life
on the plantation.

HARRIET: The older children were
already working in the fields.
My mother was cook at the Big House.
My father picked cotton or
worked in the piney woods.

2ND GIRL: "Some day," her mother said,
"we will be free.
The master promised me."

HARRIET: I thought very little
about being free.
I thought this was the way
things had to be:
Some people lived in fine houses,
had carriages with horses;
the rest of us lived in cabins
and worked on the plantation,
always in fear of the overseer
who would snap a whip with leather thongs.

1ST BOY: When Harriet turned six,
the master decided she was
strong enough to work for money.
He hired her out to a lady
to take care of her baby
and clean the house.

HARRIET: She was not a kind lady.
She used to whip my legs
when I was slow or
when I looked out of the window.

3RD GIRL: One day Harriet was so tired
she fell asleep rocking the baby.
The lady sent her back to the Big House.
Harriet cried with joy
to be back home again.

CHORUS: *Sings "Swing Low, Sweet Chariot."*

2ND BOY: The master said,
"You're strong for your age.
You'll be a good field hand."

HARRIET: Field work was not easy—
Picking cotton, cotton, cotton all day,
with the sun burning down
sometimes making me dizzy.
But I was glad to be with my people again.
When the overseer could not hear us,
we would talk and sing.

CHORUS: *Sings "My Lord, What a Morning."*

3RD BOY: Often the talk was about freedom,
a word that sounded like music
to Harriet.

HARRIET: By the time I was twelve,
I was handling a plow.
Sometimes when the master
was in need of money,
he rented my father and me out
to work for a neighbor.

1ST BOY: They cut trees,
trimmed off the branches,
and skidded the logs to the loading place.

HARRIET: When I was fifteen,
a black man who was free
came to work on the plantation
for pay.
His name was John Tubman.
We liked to work together.
After a time, John and I
got married. But in a few
months, we were not getting along well.

We didn't agree
on the one great thought
that burned in my heart:
FREEDOM!

CHORUS: *Sings "Go Down, Moses."*

1ST GIRL: John had his papers—
He was already free.
He didn't worry about Harriet
longing for freedom.

HARRIET: Suddenly, life changed again for me.
The master died and
all the slaves on the plantation
worried about what would happen:
Would we get a cruel, new master?
Would we be sold?
Would our families be separated?
The master had promised my mother
her freedom, but he died
before he signed the papers.
What would happen to us?

1ST BOY: They often heard of a
slave escaping from
one of the plantations.
Sometimes a slave would make
his way north to safety.
Sometimes slave-catchers
and their dogs
picked up the trail,
caught him, and

brought him back
to be flogged.

HARRIET: Oh, I knew the dangers,
yet the thought of freedom
was always with me,
glowing like the North Star.
One night, without telling anyone,
I took my brother's shoes
and my father's coat,
put some victuals in a sack,
and headed for the swamp.

CHORUS: *Sings "O, Shenandoah!"*

2ND BOY: Part of Maryland
near Chesapeake Bay
where the plantation lay
was swampy lowland,
with heavy timber and
thick tangles of brush
and rotting logs.

3RD GIRL: Harriet had to push through
this wet, unfriendly country,
away from roads where slave-catchers
might be lurking.
She had to travel by night
with no map to follow,
only the North Star to guide her
to the Promised Land.

HARRIET: If I could get to Philadelphia,

I knew I would be safe.
I was headed for a farm that
welcomed runaway slaves.

CHORUS: *Sings "My Lord, What a Morning."*

3RD BOY: Early on the second morning,
she reached the farm.
She was weary and splattered with mud.
They took her in, fed her, and
gave her dry clothes.
They showed her a place to hide
in the barn under the hay.

HARRIET: They told me where the next
house was on the way
to Philadelphia. "Now you're
on the Underground Railroad,"
they said.

2ND GIRL: The Underground Railroad
was a secret system to
help slaves reach the
free states and Canada.

1ST BOY: One farmer
gave her a ride in his wagon
under a load of corn.
Another farmer, a free black man,
gave her men's clothes to wear.

3RD GIRL: Finally, after many grueling days,
she reached Philadelphia,
where she found refuge

in the home of a Quaker
who ran a "station" on the Underground.
He sent her on to the home
of another Quaker
where she would be safe.

CHORUS: *Sings "Nobody Knows the Trouble I've Seen."*

HARRIET: My new mistress
was kind in every way.
She taught me
the things I should know
about doing housework,
and she paid me in cash.

I saved my money so I could go back south
to rescue my family and friends.
Oh, I knew it was dangerous.
There was a reward posted
for my capture,
a reward of thousands of dollars
for me, dead or alive!

But I knew I had been chosen
to be a second Moses,
to lead my people to freedom.

CHORUS: *Sings "Go Down, Moses."*

HARRIET: "Go down, Moses," I sang my own words.
"Go down, Moses,
Way down in Maryland.
Tell the old masters
to let my people go!"

3RD BOY: In all, Harriet went back south
            nineteen times.
            She led more than three hundred
            of her people
            from slavery to freedom,
            without ever being caught
            or losing a "passenger"
            on the Underground Railroad.

HARRIET: The hardest trip
            was the one I made
            to fetch my old mother and father.
            They were weary and the way
            was long.
            Slave-catchers watched for "Moses"
            at every crossroad.
            We had many narrow escapes.
            But we finally reached
            our promised land—
            the little house I had
            bought in New York state.
            There we found the freedom
            I had dreamed of
            for so long. . . .

CHORUS: *Sings "Swing Low, Sweet Chariot," or any
            other spiritual.*

THE END

Mary McLeod Bethune, Dream Maker

by Mary Satchell

Characters

MARY MCLEOD BETHUNE
BERTHA MITCHELL, *Mary's friend and secretary*
ROSE KEMP, *college freshman*
EMMA WILSON, *Mary's first teacher and mentor*
THOMAS, *student in Mary's first class*
MR. HILL, *Thomas's father*
ALICE JACKSON, *student at Kindell Institute*
REV. WATKINS, *principal of Kindell Institute*
BOY }
GIRL } *students in class*
STUDENTS, *six or more, as desired*

SCENE 1

TIME: *1954; Graduation Day and the Fiftieth Anniversary of Bethune-Cookman College.*
SETTING: *Mary Bethune's office at Bethune-Cookman College in Daytona Beach, Florida. Desk and chair are placed downstage, center. A phone, letter opener, and two or three stacks of mail are on desk. At left is a*

*small bookcase filled with books. Two chairs are op-
posite desk, a small table is near exit at right.*
AT RISE: MARY BETHUNE *sits at desk, opening and
reading telegrams and letters.* BERTHA MITCHELL *enters, carrying maroon cap and gown, and pauses near
table.*

BERTHA *(Scolding mildly):* Why, Mary Bethune, how
can you work at a time like this? The graduation exer-
cises will begin in little more than an hour. *(Places cap
and gown on table)* The seniors are already lining up in
front of the auditorium.

MARY *(Continuing to open mail):* This isn't work,
Bertha. I'm having the time of my life reading these
beautiful messages from my friends all over the world.
It's hard to believe that we've been running this college for 50 years.

BERTHA *(Coming to stand near desk):* We're going to
have lovely weather for today's graduation. There's not
a cloud in sight.

MARY *(Putting down letter opener):* I gave some thought
to having this year's program outside, but then I remembered what happened on our thirty-fifth anniversary.

BERTHA: Wasn't that the year Mrs. Eleanor Roosevelt
came down to be our guest speaker?

MARY *(Nodding and leaning back in her chair):* How
could I forget! We had hundreds of chairs set up on the
campus lawn, and the moment Mrs. Roosevelt stood
up to speak, it started raining.

BERTHA: What *I'll* never forget is how you walked to
Mrs. Roosevelt's side and held an umbrella over her
head while she gave her entire address.

MARY *(Mischievously):* She didn't see me glaring at the
audience, daring them to move from their seats. *(She
and BERTHA laugh.)*

BERTHA: I can laugh about that rainy graduation day now, but I certainly didn't feel like laughing then.

MARY *(Reminiscing):* I was thinking back to the year you started working as my secretary. Booker T. Washington paid his first visit to our school that same year. It was in 1908.

BERTHA *(Sitting in chair):* I remember it very well, Mary.

MARY: I'm afraid you didn't have much faith in me or my dreams in those days. *(Chuckling)* You were embarrassed because we had only one building to show Mr. Washington.

BERTHA *(Laughing at herself):* And that wasn't even finished. *(With broad sweep of her arm)* If only Mr. Washington could see it today: a four-year college with nineteen buildings! (ROSE KEMP *appears at exit, hesitates.*)

MARY *(Motioning* ROSE *to enter):* Don't stand there looking as if you're meeting the enemy, young lady. Everyone's welcome here. (ROSE *enters, appearing uncomfortable as she clutches a notepad.*)

ROSE *(Hesitantly):* Mrs. Bethune, my name is Rose Kemp, and I'd like to interview you this afternoon, if I may.

MARY *(Amused):* Who sent you, Rose? From the look on your face, you didn't come here on your own.

ROSE *(Eagerly):* I volunteered for this assignment, Mrs. Bethune. You see, I'm a freshman, and I want to make the campus newspaper staff, but the editor says I don't have what it takes to be a reporter.

MARY *(Indignantly):* I'm glad you didn't let yourself be discouraged by that kind of talk.

ROSE: I thought if I could get an interview with you, the editor might change his mind.

BERTHA *(Standing up):* Excuse me, Mrs. Bethune, but

in a little while you'll have to start greeting your guests.

MARY: Surely we can make time for something as important as a young student's future. (*Smiles at* ROSE) I think Rose and I may have a lot in common. We both have the spirit to show others what we can do.

BERTHA (*Reluctantly*): Very well. Only fifteen or twenty minutes, though, please, Mrs. Bethune, or your entire schedule will be ruined.

MARY: Much can be done in fifteen minutes. (*Kindly*) Now, Rose, if you keep your questions short and to the point, I'm sure we'll both make our deadlines.

BERTHA (*Resigned*): I should have known better than to say anything. You've never refused to give any student your time.

MARY: This is what I've lived and worked for all these years, Bertha. I can't stop now. (BERTHA *exits. To* ROSE, *humorously*) I can always tell when my assistant is annoyed with me. She calls me *Mrs. Bethune*. (ROSE *laughs and relaxes.*) Sit down, Rose, and ask whatever you wish. I'm always ready to talk. (ROSE *sits on edge of chair and holds her pen poised over pad.*)

ROSE: How did you get started as a teacher, Mrs. Bethune?

MARY: That question could take all day to answer. I didn't want to be a teacher, not at first.

ROSE (*Surprised and interested*): Really? What did you want to be?

MARY: I wanted to be a missionary, Rose. And do you know, I think I got my heart's desire. (*With mounting excitement*) Let me tell you something of my adventure, Rose. And we won't worry about the time, just now. (ROSE *begins to write, as curtain closes.*)

* * * * *

SCENE 2

TIME: *1896.*

SETTING: *The Presbyterian Mission School in Mayes-ville, South Carolina. At center, teacher's desk and chair face a long, wooden table—with several books and old-fashioned writing slate on it—and a bench with a student's jacket lying on it. Paper, pen and globe are on desk. Exit is right.*

AT RISE: MARY *tidies schoolroom. She stacks a few books from table on her desk, then goes back to bench and picks up jacket.* EMMA WILSON *comes into door-way, and seeing* MARY, *enters.*

EMMA *(Lightly):* Mary McLeod, when will you stop working and go home? Don't you ever get tired of this place?

MARY *(Surprised):* Tired of school? Good heavens, no! *(Looks around with pleasure)* This is where I come whenever I'm weary and need to be refreshed. Teaching never tires me, Miss Wilson. *(Hangs jacket over back of her chair)*

EMMA *(Laughing):* Mary, you remind me so much of myself when I started teaching. Such enthusiasm and excitement! When you first walked into my classroom so many years ago, I knew instinctively you were going to be my best student.

MARY: You had such confidence in me, Miss Wilson; I just had to live up to your expectations.

EMMA *(Becoming thoughtful, then seriously):* Mary, you've done such wonderful things for the children in this community. I've taught here in Mayesville for a long time, and I've never been as close to these young-sters as you've become in a single year.

MARY: Thank you, Miss Wilson. Your opinion of my work is very important to me.

EMMA: I know that, Mary. *(Hesitating)* And I . . . I don't want you to be discouraged by some of the gossip you may soon hear.

MARY *(Puzzled):* What gossip, Miss Wilson?

EMMA *(Forcing a smile):* I'm sure it's nothing, dear. You see, I've grown into something of a worrywart over the years, but this little community is set in its ways.

MARY *(Shaking head):* You don't have to remind me of that, Miss Wilson. I was born and raised here.

EMMA: Of course, you understand the people well, Mary. Probably better than I ever will. *(Voice borders on anger.)* But there's just no pleasing some folk!

MARY *(Sitting at desk):* Miss Wilson, I sense that you're trying to tell me something. Have I done anything wrong?

EMMA *(Laughing harshly):* Oh, Mary, no. *(Moves quickly to desk, and stands in front of it)* Why, my dear, you're just about the best thing that's ever happened to this place. You're a young, bright teacher who loves and understands these children.

MARY: Then what is it? What's gone wrong?

EMMA *(Pausing):* Some parents are complaining that you're putting new-fangled ideas in their children's heads. (MARY *remains quietly attentive.*) Many children don't want to stay and work on the farm any more. Since you've become their teacher, they talk about getting more schooling and, perhaps, leaving town.

MARY: What's wrong with that? *(Touching globe)* I've told my students this is a big world, and Mayesville is only a very tiny part of it. I want my children to know they can earn a good place for themselves in this world.

EMMA: I understand that, Mary, but some of their parents are afraid of your ideas. They don't have the faith in their children that you do.

MARY *(Rising; with determination):* I believe my students can be anything they want to be, Miss Wilson. And I will not rest till they believe it, too.

EMMA *(Gently):* I know, Mary, but sometimes we may have to bend a little in order to get the results we want. *(Touches* MARY's *shoulder)* You're still very young and idealistic.

MARY *(Firmly):* I know in my heart that I'm right, Miss Wilson, no matter what others may think.

EMMA *(Sighing):* We'll be thankful for Mary McLeod one day, for sure. *(Knock at door is heard.)*

MARY: Come in. (THOMAS *enters shyly and takes off cap.)*

THOMAS: I'm sorry to bother you, Miss McLeod, but I forgot my jacket.

MARY *(Cheerfully):* Why, Thomas, I was going to bring you your jacket this afternoon. *(Hands jacket to* THOMAS)

THOMAS *(Embarrassed):* I don't think you should stop by my house, Miss McLeod. My papa may not make you feel welcome.

EMMA *(Moving closer to* THOMAS): Is your father at home now?

THOMAS: I don't know, Miss Wilson. I turned around and came back for my jacket before I got home. Papa usually won't stop working until dinnertime.

EMMA: Your father works very hard, Thomas. And he's a good father.

THOMAS: I know that, Miss Wilson. *(Dejectedly)* Sometimes, though, I wish he could understand . . .

MARY: Understand what, Thomas?

THOMAS *(Frowning):* Papa wants me to be a farmer, but

I want to be a doctor. He says I'm just dreaming of
things that can never come true.

MARY: And I say your dreams can and *will* come true,
Thomas, if you're willing to work hard enough.

THOMAS *(Bewildered):* But, Miss McLeod, you say one
thing, and my papa says another. How can I tell who's
right?

EMMA *(Kindly):* Thomas, you must follow your own
heart whenever you have to make a hard decision.

THOMAS: Then I'll become a doctor.

MARY *(Smiling):* You have the ability to be an excellent
doctor. (MR. HILL *strides through doorway, startling
everyone.* THOMAS *looks apprehensively at his father.*
MARY *tries to be friendly.)* Good afternoon, Mr. Hill.

MR. HILL *(Gruffly):* I didn't come to pay a social call,
Miss McLeod. (*To* THOMAS) I knew you'd be here.
Why didn't you come straight home as I told you?
We've got a lot of work to do.

MARY: Thomas left his jacket, Mr. Hill, and came back to
get it. Please don't be angry with him.

MR. HILL *(Ignoring her):* Tom, go on home now. I'll be
there in a minute.

THOMAS: Yes, sir. *(Exits quickly)*

MR. HILL *(Scowling at* MARY): I resent your putting all
those useless notions in my son's head. Instead of
working on the farm, he wants to become a doctor!

EMMA: Mr. Hill, I think you're being unfair to Miss
McLeod.

MR. HILL: I knew Mary McLeod's parents before she
was born. They're not ashamed to be farmers.

MARY *(Struggling for patience):* I'm proud of what my
parents have achieved, and they *encouraged* me to go
to school and be a teacher.

MR. HILL (*Stubbornly*): Maybe Sam McLeod let his daughter have her way, but my son's going to be a farmer, and that's final!

MARY: Mr. Hill, is it fair to force your child to be something he doesn't want to be?

MR. HILL (*Pointing a finger at* MARY): I'm a lot older than you, young lady, and I've raised five children besides Thomas. I've got more experience than you in these matters.

MARY (*Resolutely*): Your son has an excellent mind. He wants to use his mind to the best of his ability.

MR. HILL: This is 1896, Mary McLeod, and a black youngster can break his heart fighting against the odds. (*Voice softens*) You may not think so, but I love my son, and I don't want to see him hurt.

EMMA: It seems you both want what's best for Thomas. At least, that's a starting point.

MR. HILL: I've got no quarrel with you, Miss Wilson. You've been the kind of teacher that Mayesville can be proud of. We need more teachers like you, and fewer troublemakers. (*Casts angry look at* MARY)

EMMA (*In a low, steady voice*): Miss McLeod is a very good teacher. In fact, I intend to recommend that she take my place as permanent teacher when I retire. (MARY, *stunned, goes to sit at her desk, and busies herself with papers.* THOMAS *suddenly re-appears at door.*)

MR. HILL (*Abruptly*): What are you doing here, Tom? (THOMAS, *holding his cap tightly, walks to his father.*)

THOMAS (*Quietly*): I've got something to tell you, Papa.

MR. HILL: It can wait, son. Your mother will be needing your help at home.

THOMAS (*Determined*): I have to tell you now. (MARY,

concerned, stands up.)

MARY *(Quickly breaking in):* Is there anything I can do, Thomas?

THOMAS: No, Miss McLeod. I've made up my mind to quit school right away. *(Adults look stunned.)*

MR. HILL *(Angrily):* What kind of foolish talk is that? You can't stop going to school. I won't hear of it.

THOMAS *(Confused):* But, you said you didn't want me to go to school.

MR. HILL *(Impatiently):* I said no such thing. I want you to be a farmer, and farmers need to know as much as they can. They have to run a business.

THOMAS *(Tearfully):* It seems I can never please you, no matter how hard I try. *(Shoulders sag, sighs dejectedly)* All right, Papa, I'll do as you say, but don't blame Miss McLeod. She only tried to help. *(Head down,* THOMAS *moves slowly right.)*

MR. HILL *(Starting after* TOM): Tom, son, wait— (THOMAS *exits without looking back.* MR. HILL *looks at others in bewilderment.)* I never saw my boy look so hurt before. All his spirit seems to be gone.

EMMA: Maybe I can talk to him. *(Exits hurriedly)*

MR. HILL *(Glancing anxiously at* MARY): I didn't mean to do this to him. *(Sits on bench worriedly)*

MARY *(Earnestly):* Mr. Hill, how many of your children are still living at home?

MR. HILL: Three. Tom is the youngest and the smartest, I have to admit.

MARY: Our little school can hold only so many students, and most families in Mayesville are quite large. I plan to ask the parents to let me teach their youngest children year round.

MR. HILL *(Thinking it over; slowly):* Only the youngest?

MARY: I'll promise to let the others work the farms, and

maybe someday we'll have a school big enough for all the children.

MR. HILL: You're one smart lady, Miss McLeod. I guess I can't refuse your offer, since we'll be left with two kids to help out when Tom's in school.

MARY: I'll certainly be back to get your other two, but that will take a while. (*They laugh.* MR. HILL *rises.*)

MR. HILL: I apologize, Miss McLeod. Emma Wilson was right. You *are* a good teacher. You do care about these kids, and I'm going to see to it that all my neighbors find out what you're doing for us.

MARY: And what about your boy's future?

MR. HILL (*Sincerely*): Miss McLeod, you've convinced me that my son should get all the schooling he can. (*Pausing*) If he wants to be a doctor, I think he ought to have the chance.

MARY (*Gratefully*): Thank you, Mr. Hill. (*Puts out her hand*) I know Thomas will make you very proud. (*They shake hands.*)

MR. HILL: Good day, ma'am. (*Puts on hat, exits.* MARY *stands thoughtfully for a moment, then returns to desk and absently studies the globe.* EMMA *enters, excitedly.*)

EMMA: Mary McLeod, how on earth did you perform this miracle? Mr. Hill is a changed man! And I never saw a happier child than Tom when his father told him he could try to be a doctor. (*Goes to* MARY; *solemnly*) How do you feel about teaching here permanently? You know I must retire soon.

MARY: Thank you for your confidence in me, Miss Wilson, but I can't spend the rest of my life in Mayesville.

EMMA (*Greatly disappointed*): Why, Mary, has all this talk made you want to leave us?

MARY: No, that had nothing to do with my decision, Miss Wilson. I guess I've always known, deep down, that I'd have to move on someday.

EMMA: Are you sure you're not making a mistake, Mary?

MARY: I don't know. I only know that something is pulling me toward my destiny.

EMMA *(Sadly):* How soon do you plan to leave? *(Quietly)* And how will we tell Thomas?

MARY: I'll stay here and teach for a few more years. Thomas will be all right.

EMMA *(With concern):* Mary, where will you go?

MARY *(Confidently):* I don't know yet what I'm to do with my life, but one thing I'm sure of, I *must* keep searching until I find out. *(Curtain)*

* * * * *

SCENE 3

TIME: *A few years later.*

SETTING: *Classroom at Kindell Institute in Sumter, South Carolina. Mary McLeod Bethune's desk and chair are up left, opposite two or three rows of her students' old-fashioned desks. A wastebasket and lectern stand beside Mary's desk, which has books and globe on it. Exit is right.*

AT RISE: ALICE JACKSON *somberly enters, carrying books, which she puts inside her desk. She goes to* MARY's *desk and plays with the globe absently, slowly spinning it as she leans against the desk.* MARY *enters unnoticed, and studies the girl before speaking.*

MARY *(Brightly):* Why, Alice, you're certainly the early bird today. The rest of your family must still be at the breakfast table. *(Takes off shawl and drapes it over back of her chair)*

ALICE *(Glancing curiously at* MARY*)*: I don't have a family, Mrs. Bethune. My parents died a long time ago. I live at the Children's Home.

MARY *(Sadly)*: Goodness, you're only a young girl, and you talk as if you're older than I am.

ALICE: But it's true. *(Sadly)* I wish I did have a family like the other children here at school.

MARY *(Putting hand on* ALICE*'s shoulder)*: Alice, I think you should count your blessings. Why, you're far more fortunate than many of your classmates.

ALICE *(Shaking head)*: How can you say that, Mrs. Bethune?

MARY: You have a very large family at the Children's Home. There are people at that orphanage who love and care for you just as parents do. If you look at it that way, every boy and girl at the Children's Home is really your brother and sister.

ALICE: I hadn't thought of it like that. (ALICE *turns back to globe and spins it.)*

MARY: That globe was given to me when I graduated from Scotia Seminary years ago. *(Enthusiastically)* I've kept it since as a reminder of how big and wonderful this world is.

ALICE *(Mockingly)*: It looks very tiny to me, Mrs. Bethune. *(Puts finger on one spot of globe)* See? I can cover up a whole island with just one of my fingers.

MARY *(Amused)*: You know this globe is only on a very small scale, Alice. Of course, we all know that in reality, our world is extremely large, and you mustn't forget it. Never limit your future or your dreams.

ALICE *(Moving from desk)*: Mrs. Bethune, I used to

dream of being adopted and having a mother and father of my own. *(Wistfully)* We would live in our own
house; I'd have clothes as nice as the other girls at
school. I waited a long time for someone to come to the
orphanage and take me home. *(Looks down at her
shoes)* But nobody ever came.

MARY *(Putting her arm around* ALICE's *shoulder):* Perhaps you should change your dream a little. *I* did,
when I was about twenty years old. You see, I didn't
really want to be a schoolteacher.

ALICE *(Shyly):* You're the best teacher I ever had, Mrs.
Bethune.

MARY: When I hear one of my students say that, I'm
glad I had to change my dream of being a missionary.
Teachers get the chance to help so many people.

ALICE *(Shyly):* I hope someday I can help a lot of people.
(Other students enter, carrying books. They greet
MARY, *take seats, and put books in desks.* ALICE *goes
to her seat.* MARY *goes to her desk and sits.)*

MARY *(Cheerfully):* Good morning, everyone. We're
going to begin our class a little differently today. I'd
like you to talk about your secret dreams—what you
would *really* like to be when you grow up. Who wants
to start? *(Silence. Finally,* BOY *raises his hand.)* Yes?

BOY: I want to be a preacher like our principal, Reverend
Watkins.

GIRL *(Smirking):* Humph! You're too bad to be a minis-
ter. *(All laugh.)*

MARY *(Reproachfully):* I don't want to hear any more of
that. *(Glances casually at class, then lets her eyes rest
on* ALICE*)* Alice, what's your secret dream?

ALICE *(Caught offguard):* Well . . . *(Very softly)* I want
to be a nurse.

STUDENTS *(From opposite side of the class; ad lib):* Talk louder, Alice. We can't hear you. *(Etc.)*

ALICE *(Loudly and defiantly):* I want to be a nurse.

MARY *(Gently, firmly):* Then it's settled, Alice. That's what you will be.

ALICE: But I live at the Children's Home, Mrs. Bethune. How could I ever get to nursing school?

MARY *(Decisively, leaving her desk):* We'll talk about that as soon as I get back. Excuse me for a moment, class. *(Exits rapidly)*

BOY *(Threateningly, turning to* GIRL): So I'm too bad to be a preacher, am I? *(He gets a slingshot from his desk.)*

STUDENTS *(Ad lib):* I dare you. Leave her alone! *(Etc.)*

GIRL *(Fearfully):* You'd better not do that! I'll tell Mrs. Bethune! (MARY *re-enters, briskly;* BOY *quickly hides slingshot.* REV. WATKINS *enters, follows* MARY *to her desk. Class quickly quiets down.)*

MARY *(Standing behind desk):* Class, I asked Reverend Watkins to tell you a little about his life, especially his youth. *(To* REV. WATKINS) Reverend, we'd like to hear about your childhood, and how you came to be a school principal. *(Sits at desk)*

WATKINS *(Standing at lectern; to* MARY): Thank you, Mrs. Bethune. *(To class)* Good morning, boys and girls. *(Gives a little bow)*

STUDENTS *(Together):* Good morning, Reverend Watkins.

WATKINS: I didn't expect to be making a speech so early, but I'm always glad to talk to our students. *(Takes off glasses, wipes them with handkerchief, then puts them on again)* Mrs. Bethune tells me you've been talking about your plans for the future. My future seemed pretty dismal when I was your age. *(Sighs)* You see, I was an orphan, and I lived at the Children's Home right here in town. (ALICE, *shocked, leans forward.*) But I wanted to be something in life, to get an education, and to help others.

ALICE: You must have been adopted by rich people who could send you away to college.

WATKINS *(Smiling):* That was my secret dream for over twelve years, Alice. However, nobody ever came to adopt me, either rich or poor. I stayed at the Children's Home till I was old enough to go out on my own. I took any job I could get to finish college.

ALICE *(With awe):* You came from the Children's Home, Reverend Watkins, and yet your dreams came true?

WATKINS *(Assertively):* I *made* my dreams come true, young lady, and so can all of you.

MARY *(Graciously):* Thank you. You've been a great help to us, Reverend Watkins.

WATKINS: Please invite me again, and next time, I'll spend more time with you. *(Bowing to* MARY*)* And before I go, I think the class would like to ask you about *your* secret dream, Mrs. Bethune. *(Turns to class)* Isn't that right? *(Students nod their heads and clap their hands.)*

MARY *(Flustered):* I didn't expect the tables to be turned this way. *(Laughs lightly)* Yet I suppose it's only fair.

BOY: Mrs. Bethune, I'll bet you want to be a principal like Rev. Watkins.

MARY: You're getting warm, but not quite. What I really want to do is establish a college one day. My son Albert, Jr. is just an infant, but I want to see him in a good college when he's old enough. And I want to see every other youngster get the same opportunity.

WATKINS *(Sincerely):* I have no doubt that you will build your college, Mrs. Bethune. It's just a matter of time. My only regret is that you'll be leaving us someday.

MARY: My husband said there may be some opportunity for us in Florida. A new railroad's being built on the east coast of the state, and we plan to visit there soon.

WATKINS: I wish you well, Mrs. Bethune. Some of my friends live in Daytona Beach. I hope you'll find time to look them up.

MARY: It will be my pleasure, Reverend Watkins. *(With fervor)* Wherever my journey may lead me, I'm sure I'll spend the rest of my days in helping students like these to have happier and better lives. *(Curtain)*

* * * * *

EPILOGUE

TIME: *1954.*

SETTING: *Same as in Scene 1.*

AT RISE: MARY *sits, holding mortarboard and graduation robe.* ROSE *holds notepad.*

MARY: So then, Rose, my family and I moved here to Daytona Beach, and I opened my tiny school in 1904. (ROSE *jots down some notes.*) There were only five students at the time. In 1923, my school for girls was combined with a boys' school, Cookman Institute of Jacksonville.

ROSE *(Proudly):* And now Bethune-Cookman College has over 1,300 students.

MARY *(Smiling radiantly):* Yes. So you see, Rose, my life has been a grand adventure, and I honestly can say that it still is an adventure.

ROSE *(Scribbling rapidly on notepad):* That's a beautiful quote to end my feature article with, Mrs. Bethune.

(With great enthusiasm) This is going to be one of the
best stories ever printed in our college newspaper.

MARY: I'm eager to read it. *(Shakes a finger at* ROSE*)*
Just you be sure to quote me correctly and get all the
facts straight.

ROSE: Oh, I will! I can't afford to make any mistakes. It
will give me the chance I need. My career in jour-
nalism may depend on how this article turns out.

MARY: Nonsense, your career *and* your future would
hardly depend on one little incident. What you become
depends largely on what you *do*, hour after hour, day
after day, year after year. (MARY *picks up robe.*)

ROSE: Please let me help you with that, Mrs. Bethune.
(Helps MARY *put on robe)*

MARY: Thank you, my dear. *(Facing* ROSE*)* Now that we
have only a few moments left together, I'll ask you a
question, Rose. You've asked me so many.

ROSE *(Flippantly):* Fire away!

MARY: Just what is your secret dream?

ROSE *(A bit defensively):* Why would you want to know
that, Mrs. Bethune?

MARY: I always get around to asking that of every young
person I meet. Give me an answer quickly. (BERTHA
enters right.)

BERTHA *(Anxiously):* The program's about to begin. All
the seniors are in line and ready to march into the
auditorium. Please hurry, Mary. Everyone's waiting
for you.

MARY: I'll be there in a moment, Bertha. (BERTHA *exits,
and "Pomp and Circumstance" begins to play softly
offstage.)*

ROSE *(Evasively):* We don't have time to talk any longer,
Mrs. Bethune. The music has started.

MARY *(Persistently):* Oh yes, we do, Rose. I won't budge until you tell me.

ROSE *(Relenting):* All right. I really dream of publishing my own weekly newspaper.

MARY: Promise me you won't stop until you reach your goal.

ROSE *(Vowing solemnly):* I promise that, one day, I'll have my own newspaper. *(Strains of graduation music grow louder.)*

MARY *(Adjusting mortarboard):* Now, it's time to go. We'll meet again at this same place three years from today, Rose. I'll present you the college newspaper editor's award at your graduation. Is that a deal?

ROSE *(Happily):* Yes, Mrs. Bethune. It's a deal! *(They exit. MARY, with head high, leads the way. Music grows louder, and continues to end of march. Curtain)*

THE END

PRODUCTION NOTES

MARY MCLEOD BETHUNE: DREAM MAKER

Characters: 4 male; 6 female. Six or more additional boys and girls for classroom scene.

Playing Time: 30 minutes.

Costumes: Scene 1: Mary Bethune is a dignified older woman with gray hair. She wears conservative jacket dress and single strand of pearls. Bertha and Rose wear clothes appropriate for the mid 1950s. Scene 2: Traditional late 19th century dress. Women may wear long-sleeved blouses and ankle-length skirts. Mary is a young woman. Emma's hair is graying. Thomas and Mr. Hill wear farmer's clothes. Mr. Hill wears battered wide-brimmed hat, and Thomas has a cap and jacket. Scene 3: Alice wears a faded calico or homespun-type dress. Mary wears short cape or shawl. Reverend Watkins wears dark suit with frock coat and high collared shirt, and glasses.

Properties: Cap and gown, notepad, pen, papers, books, glasses, handkerchief, slingshot.

Setting: Scene 1: Mary Bethune's office. Mary's desk and chair are down center. A phone, letter opener and two or three stacks of mail are on desk. At left is a small bookcase filled with books. Two chairs are opposite desk, and small table is near exit at right. Scene 2: A little rural schoolroom. A teacher's desk and chair face a long wooden table and bench. Some books, and an old-fashioned writing slate are on table. Paper, pen and a globe of the earth are on desk. Exit is right. Scene 3: Larger classroom. Mary's desk and chair are upstage left, opposite two or three rows of old-fashioned desks. A wastebasket and lectern stand beside desk, which holds a few books supported by bookends and the globe. Exit is right. Epilogue: Same as Scene 1.

Sound: Graduation music, as indicated in text.

Abe Lincoln and
the Runaways

by Wenta Jean Watson

Characters

CALLIE } *runaway slaves*
BIG JIM }
MR. TANDY
JUDGE ROLLINS
ABE LINCOLN
HIRAM
TEACHER
LEE
MATILDA
ELIZA
PHOEBE

TIME: *Early fall, 1822.*
BEFORE RISE: BIG JIM *and* CALLIE, *carrying sack, run
    in from right. They stop and look around cautiously.*
CALLIE: I'm tired, Big Jim. We just can't outrun them.
BIG JIM: Callie, we came a long way from that planta-
    tion. I don't know what's ahead, but I have a dream of
    living free and of raising my children free, and if I have
    to run till I drop, then that's the way it's going to be!
CALLIE *(Looking off right):* I hear them coming. Where
    are we going to hide?

BIG JIM *(Looking around, then pointing off left):* Behind that rock. Hurry. *(He takes her hand, and they exit left.* MR. TANDY *and* JUDGE ROLLINS *enter from right, carrying riding crops.)*

JUDGE: They have to be near here. They can't get any farther on foot.

MR. TANDY: There's a search party out looking for them now, Judge Rollins. They'll find your slaves soon.

JUDGE: They'd better. I have to leave tomorrow. My ship for France sails next week. I'll give the searchers double what I offered them. If those slaves get away, others will try to escape, too.

MR. TANDY: With double reward money I can assure you that the runaways will be found.

JUDGE: I hate to lose them. Big Jim is a good worker, and his sister Callie is the best cook I've ever had. *(Rubs his stomach)* If we find them in time, Callie can fix a good meal for me before I have to leave. *(They exit left. After a few moments,* BIG JIM *and* CALLIE *enter from left, look around cautiously.)*

BIG JIM *(Wiping his brow):* That was a close call.

CALLIE *(Taking two apples out of sack, and handing one to* BIG JIM*):* We ought to eat something.

BIG JIM: All right, but we have to keep moving while we eat. No time to stop. *(They start off left.)*

CALLIE: Where are we going to hide till dark?

BIG JIM: From up on the hill I spied a schoolhouse. After the children go home, we'll get in through an open window and stay there. There won't be anybody around.

CALLIE: It will be good to rest, and a school will be safe.

BIG JIM: I hope so, Callie. But we can't even trust a child—catching runaways means money, you know. Let's go. *(They exit left.)*

*　*　*　*　*

SETTING: *Indiana. Log cabin schoolhouse with steps and working door is center. Large window is on right side of house; bench stands near it. Several logs of various sizes are scattered around in front of bench.*

AT RISE: ABE *is seated on one step; facing him on another step is* HIRAM. *Both are reading books.* ABE *is mumbling the words out loud.* BIG JIM *sneaks in right, unnoticed by* ABE *and* HIRAM, *and crosses to bench. He places bench beneath window, climbs up on it and peers inside schoolhouse, then ducks down and waits.*

HIRAM: Abe . . . *(There is no answer.)* Abraham! . . . *(Still no response)* Abraham!!

ABE *(Looking up):* Yes, Hiram?

HIRAM: I wish you wouldn't read out loud.

ABE: I like to listen to the sound of the words. Seems I can remember them better if I speak them. (TEACHER *comes out of schoolhouse door and looks at boys.* ABE *continues to read out loud.* BIG JIM *peers in through window again and then motions offstage to* CALLIE, *who enters.* BIG JIM *climbs into school through window and leans out to help* CALLIE. *She drops sack on ground, gives one hand to* BIG JIM *and holds her skirt up with other. After they are inside, she leans out to get sack, but* BIG JIM *pulls her back quickly.)*

TEACHER *(To* ABE): Are you both going to stay here, Abe?

ABE: Sir, I thought I would do some reading in *Pilgrim's Progress* before I go home. I have lots of chores to do before bedtime, and it's hard to read by lamp light.

HIRAM: I don't do chores. When I get home, I go straight to the stables to look at that big bay Pa bought at the auction last month. We plan to race him and make lots of money.

TEACHER: I'm proud of both of you.

ABE: Ma sets great store by learning and tells me to
keep at it.

TEACHER: It's the key to the world.

ABE: I've seen some educated fellers that don't impress
me much. I'd say they were educated fools.

TEACHER *(Pointing to heart):* It's what's in here that
counts. But you have to use your head along with it.
(Pauses) Our nation is growing all the time. People are
pushing West every day. There will be new states
joining the Union and opportunities for educated men
to represent them in Washington. You keep on with
the studying, and someday you might be two of the
men responsible for decision-making in this country.

HIRAM: Do you suppose slavery will be allowed in the
West? There is a great deal of talk for and against it.

TEACHER: I don't know. There is much dissension over
the question throughout the land. The North gener-
ally opposes it, but the economy of the South is built
on slavery.

ABE: I don't think it's right for one man to own another,
as if he were property.

HIRAM: I wager that if your father had the money he
would buy a field hand.

ABE: I don't think so. Pa had trouble with land deeds in
Kentucky, but I think one reason we moved here to
Indiana was to get away from slavery.

TEACHER: Someday the disagreement over slavery may
come close to tearing our Union apart.

HIRAM: What do you mean?

TEACHER: War may eventually have to settle the issue. I
hate to think of it. If the North and South clash, it will
take a giant of a man to lead the country and to keep it
together.

HIRAM: I'd like to be that man. Father and Mother say

I'm destined to be in high places. They say it's because
of the extra study I do here at school.

TEACHER: You and Abe are good students. In a few
years we'll see how you both turn out. *(Pause)* Would
one of you bring in some firewood before you go home?

HIRAM: Certainly. *(Gets up and places hands on back)*
Oh-h, I just remembered my back—I hurt it yesterday
while I was out riding. Abe can fetch the wood.

ABE *(Standing up and closing book):* I'll get it now, sir.

TEACHER: Thank you, Abe. I'll see you tomorrow. *(He
exits left. As* ABE *puts down his book,* LEE *enters
right, carrying a fish pole made of tree branch.)*

LEE: Hi, fellas. I'm going fishing. Come along.

ABE: I can't go, Lee. I have to get some wood for the
school, and then I want to do some more reading.

LEE: Just tie the fishing line around your toe, and you
can keep on with your everlasting reading, Abe.

ABE *(Shaking head):* Some other time, Lee.

LEE: How about you, Hiram?

HIRAM: No. Fishing's messy business. All those wiggly
worms! Not to mention cleaning the fish. But, if you
catch any big ones, Father will buy them from you—
that is, *if* you will clean them first.

LEE: Sorry, Hiram. Whatever I catch, I clean and eat.
(He starts to exit, then turns back.) Say, I hear there's
a party of men out looking for some runaway slaves.

HIRAM *(Excitedly):* Maybe there's a reward out!

ABE: Would you turn them in for money?

HIRAM *(Stiffly):* Yes, I would. I believe in keeping the
law. Slaves are considered property and should be
returned to their owner.

ABE: But they're not property. They're people like us.

LEE *(Laughing):* Hiram, I can see the shingle hanging
outside your law office in a few years. *(Points to imagi-*

nary sign) Hiram Scarem, Attorney-at-law. *(He laughs again and then sobers as he looks offstage.)* Uh-oh. Have to go, friends. I see the girls headed this way, and I don't want to be cornered by them. *(He exits left. From offstage right are heard sounds of laughter.)*

GIRLS *(Ad lib; calling from offstage):* Lee! You can't run away from us! *(Etc.* HIRAM *smooths his hair and sits back, while* ABE *gathers wood.* MATILDA, ELIZA, *and* PHOEBE *enter from right and start playing a game of tag.* ABE *sees sack on ground, puts down wood and looks in sack, pulls out apple, looks up at window, puts apple back, and then tosses sack inside window. He picks up wood and crosses to girls, who join hands and dance around* ABE. *As they dance, they begin chanting together.)* We're going to have a party! We're going to have a party!

MATILDA *(Dropping hands of other girls):* Eliza is going to have a candypulling Saturday night, Abe. You will come, won't you?

ABE: Thank you, Matilda, but I had my mind set on studying.

ELIZA: We won't let you escape till you say "yes." *(Girls again join hands and begin to dance around him.)*

PHOEBE: Uncle Jess is going to play his banjo for us. We'll have a dance later.

ABE *(Turning around in circle):* I'm not good at dancing, but I do like candy. I'll try to come. *(Girls unclasp hands, allowing* ABE *to take wood into schoolhouse.)*

MATILDA: Hiram, will you come?

HIRAM: I planned to pay a call on my grandmother.

ELIZA: Too bad, because my cousin Jane will be there. Her father is a Congressman.

HIRAM: A Congressman, you say? Hm-m-m. Perhaps I

could talk my brother into visiting Grandma. I
wouldn't want to disappoint a charming young lady
like you. (*He bows deeply to* ELIZA.)

ELIZA (*Looking off right*): Who are those men riding up?

MATILDA (*Also looking off*): I think it is Judge Rollins
and his overseer. (JUDGE ROLLINS *and* MR. TANDY
enter from right.)

JUDGE: Hello, children. Did you just get out of school?

PHOEBE: Yes, sir.

JUDGE: Some of you may know me. I'm Judge Rollins,
and this is my overseer, Mr. Tandy. We are visiting in
the neighborhood.

HIRAM: How do you do? (*Looks off right*) Sir, you have
mighty fine-looking horses.

JUDGE: Finest this side of the Ohio River, son.

MR. TANDY: Sir, perhaps these children have seen the
runaways. (ABE *comes to door and listens.*)

JUDGE: Could be, Mr. Tandy. (*To children*) Two of my
slaves have run off, a sister and brother. Their names
are Callie and Big Jim. Has any of you seen them?

GIRLS (*Ad lib*): No. Haven't seen them. (*Etc.*)

MR. TANDY: How about you boys?

HIRAM: We've heard about them.

ABE: Have they done anyone harm, or stolen anything?

JUDGE: No, they just up and ran off. They're my property—I pay tax on them, and I want them back.

ABE: They must have had cause to run away.

MR. TANDY: Nonsense! They want to be free—that's all.

ABE: Can't say I blame them. I wouldn't want to be
owned, the same as an animal. (*He looks at* HIRAM.) I
hear some people treat their thoroughbreds better
than their slaves. (*He comes down steps.*)

HIRAM: That's not important, Abe. Slaves are property,
pure and simple.

JUDGE *(Impatiently):* Come, come. Have you seen them?

HIRAM: Are you offering a good reward?

MR. TANDY *(Sharply):* Look here. Do you know anything about them or not?

HIRAM *(Slyly):* I sure do love good horseflesh.

JUDGE: Young man, are you trying to blackmail me out of my horses?

HIRAM: No. But if I had a horse like yours, I could find those slaves fast enough.

JUDGE: All right. You have my word that if you find my slaves, one of my fine horses will be yours. I'm staying at the inn, and you can find me there. But you have only until dawn to find them, as I have to leave town after sun-up. Come, Tandy. *(He bows to girls, then he and* MR. TANDY *exit, right.)*

HIRAM: What luck! I know this country inside and out. They must be nearby. They probably picked out a place that's right under our very noses.

PHOEBE: Surely you aren't planning to search for them, are you, Hiram?

HIRAM: My dear Phoebe, I am merely being a good citizen. If I stand to make a profit, that is my good fortune. I must get going. There aren't many daylight hours left.

ABE: Say, Hiram, I'll bet they're down by the river. They'd be hungry by now, and there are lots of fish to be caught.

HIRAM *(Snapping fingers):* You're right, Abe. I'll start there. I have to take this book inside first, though. *(He starts for steps, but* ABE *blocks his way.)*

ABE: No need, Hiram. I'm going back in. I'll take it for you.

HIRAM: Why, thanks. (*Hands book to* ABE) I want to get down to the river before it gets any darker.

ABE: Watch out for Lee. He gets a might riled if anyone disturbs his fishing.

HIRAM: He'll never know I'm around. *(He exits, left.)*

PHOEBE: I hope he doesn't find them.

ABE: Don't worry. Hiram isn't going to find the runaways.

MATILDA: Abe, why did you tell Hiram about the river?

ABE: If he had stayed here studying he might put me to shame at our spelldown tomorrow.

PHOEBE *(Laughing):* No one could ever beat you, Abe. We'll see you in school tomorrow. *(Turning)* Let's start for home, girls.

MATILDA: Do you want to walk with us, Abe?

ABE: I have to put Hiram's book away—you go on ahead. (*Girls exit, right.* ABE *looks down at book, then at schoolhouse, climbs steps and speaks loudly.*) I sure hate to go back inside. I could have sworn there were ghosts in there. (*A hand comes out through doorway and takes book.* ABE *walks down steps again and picks up his own book from the ground.*) This *Pilgrim's Progress* book is so interesting—all about a journey and the trouble a body can get into if he's not careful. Why, if I were on a trip right now, I'd be most wary about traveling at night. I'd start out after the sun comes up, when most people who have been out in the night would return to their beds, or be eating breakfast. I'd stay clear of main roads, too. *(He closes book and looks up)* Well—I'd better head for home. Ma will have supper waiting. (*Exits.* CALLIE *and* BIG JIM *come out of school.*)

BIG JIM: What a fine boy!

CALLIE: He knew we were hiding in the school, but never said one word to give us away. He could have had a reward, too. Why do you think he didn't tell on us?

BIG JIM: Don't know, Callie. Guess you can trust some people, after all.

CALLIE: He looked poor. His clothes were worn.

BIG JIM: Just the same, he is a gentleman at heart. I wish I knew his name.

CALLIE: I heard them call him Abe. Must be Abraham something.

BIG JIM *(Musing):* Abraham. That's a good name.

CALLIE: I'm never going to forget that boy. He's so tall and thin. I'll always remember it was Abraham who helped us slaves escape.

BIG JIM: I just wish he could help *all* our brothers and sisters escape. *(Pause)* We'd better get some rest while we can, Callie. Come. (*He takes her by the hand and turns to doorway.* CALLIE *looks offstage after* ABE *as lights begin to dim. "The Battle Hymn of the Republic" is played softly in background.*)

CALLIE: Our people are going to be free one day, Big Jim. I just know it. I feel it in my bones. (*She turns to go inside with* BIG JIM, *then turns once more toward audience.*) Abraham. That's a good strong name, Abraham. *(They go inside as "The Battle Hymn of the Republic" comes up loudly, perhaps with voices of choir. Curtain)*

THE END

PRODUCTION NOTES

ABE LINCOLN AND THE RUNAWAYS

Characters: 7 male; 4 female.

Playing Time: 20 minutes.

Costumes: Dark pants and shirts for Abe, Hiram, and Lee. Teacher wears suit with tie. Mr. Tandy and Judge Rollins, suits, hats and boots. Big Jim, pants, shirt, colorful bandana around neck. Callie, long dress, apron, bandana on head, and large earrings. Girls, long dresses, hair ribbons.

Properties: Two books; two riding crops; fish pole; burlap sack containing apples.

Setting: Indiana. Log cabin schoolhouse with steps and working door is center. Large window is on right side of house; bench stands near it. A wood pile with several logs of various sizes scattered around is in front of bench.

Lighting: At close of play lights dim, indicating dusk.

Music: "The Battle Hymn of the Republic."

The Abolition Flyer

by Louis Lerman

Characters

STORYTELLER
LEVI COFFIN
ARTHUR TAPPAN
WILLIAM LLOYD GARRISON } *abolitionists*
HARRIET TUBMAN
JOHN HENRY
PEOPLE
PASSENGERS } *extras*

AUTHOR'S NOTE

The Underground Railroad was the name given to the secret system of helping fugitive slaves from the South reach the free states and Canada before and during the Civil War. Beginning around 1804, fugitive slaves were taken, mostly at night, from station to station by "conductors" until they reached safety. Levi Coffin, whose home was an important station, became known as "president" of the Underground Railroad; other leaders of the movement included William Lloyd Garrison and Harriet Tubman. The legendary John Henry helped set the tracks through the Swannonoa tunnel in West Virginia, the longest and most difficult tunnel ever cut through a mountain. Many thousands of slaves—men, women, and children—rode the Underground Railroad to freedom.

STORYTELLER: In the days before the Civil War, they used to say . . .

PEOPLE: The Underground Railroad—that's Quaker Levi Coffin's road. He's president of it. Poor accommodations, but cheap traveling. The railroad runs north from anywhere below the Mason Dixon line—Florida, Georgia, Mississippi, Tennessee, the Carolinas. There was a time when it had a branch line into the Kansas Territory, built especially for John Brown. It went way up into Wendell Phillips's front parlor in Boston, Massachusetts, then across the border into Canada.

STORYTELLER: Now they tell this story:
Friend Levi Coffin
Was a railroad man
Ran the Abolition Flyer
To the promised land.

Had a locomotive engine
Nobody could see
But that Abolition Flyer
Made history

There never was
A train like that
A thousand miles
On a phantom track.

That train went riding,
Riding along
And the wheels were singing
A strange new song.

The people came
From miles around
To see that train,

To hear that song,
To ask if they could come along.

Levi's road had glory
His road had fame
For every slaver
Cursed his name.

But the road was poor
It lost money
Because Levi rode
All his passengers free!

So Levi gathered the Board of Directors at his house
in Cincinnati. Among them were Frederick Douglass
and Congressman Thaddeus Stevens and William
Lloyd Garrison and Harriet Tubman and Arthur Tappan from New York. Levi opened the meeting with a
prayer, then got down to business.

LEVI COFFIN: Friend Tappan, would thee be kind
enough to give the financial report?

ARTHUR TAPPAN: Ladies and gentlemen, members of
the board, Mr. Chairman . . . our assets to date are in
the neighborhood of fifty thousand men, women, and
children freed from slavery—including, I am proud to
say, some members of our Board present.
We're in very sound condition
With a glorious tradition
For an apparition road
We're doing very, very well.
Only trouble is, we don't have any money. Not a cent.

COFFIN: Money or no money, Friend Tappan, we must
expand. With the Fugitive Slave Law just passed by
Congress, there will be three, four hundred thousand

people waiting to travel north. It would be sinful not to take advantage of the business possibilities.

TAPPAN: You know as well as I do, Mr. Chairman, what shape the railroad is in. Coaches tumble down and engines stop. And the roadbed—well, no use even talking about that. Every slave-catcher in the United States seems to know that the stretch of road on the top of Smoky Mountain, between North Carolina and Tennessee, is bad. Can't do a thing until we get that fixed up. But where's the money going to come from?

COFFIN: The Lord will provide, Mr. Tappan.

WILLIAM LLOYD GARRISON: Is there anything *we* can do to help the Lord, Mr. Tappan?

TAPPAN: Well, we need labor. That's the big item.

COFFIN: Sister Harriet Tubman, do thee think we can get enough free labor down there to fix that stretch of road?

HARRIET TUBMAN: All we have to do is whisper we're coming, Friend Levi.

COFFIN: Friends, I propose that a small committee take a trip down and get a firsthand view of the situation.

STORYTELLER: That's the way it was decided. It was a nice, sunny day when they started out. The coaches and engine were cleaned up, oiled and greased. Harriet Tubman, with a big smile, sang out. (*Recording of train whistle and other sounds can be played in background.*)

TUBMAN:
All aboard for
Florida
Georgia
Mississippi
Tennessee

North and South
Carolina
and the Kansas-Nebraska Territory
Missouri
and all points South.

All aboard
The Abolition Flyer
Shovel the coal
Push the steam a little higher.
Wheels a'rolling
Rolling along
And the whistle blowing
That freedom song.

STORYTELLER: Engineer Coffin pulled the whistle cord
    three times. The steam started to hiss, the wheels
    started to roll, and with all the people on the platform
    yelling . . .

PEOPLE: Good luck! Good luck! Have a nice trip!

STORYTELLER: The train pulled out. The engine rolled
    along pretty well, except that every once in a while the
    firebox heated up and they had to stop and wait around
    until it cooled off. They could tell it was the South as
    soon as they hit it. Every time they stopped, even for a
    minute, there would be people around. Everyone
    seemed to know where the train was going, and how
    much a ticket cost. They just stood around, waiting for
    the train to start so they could get on board. At first,
    Harriet said:

TUBMAN: We'll pick you up on the way back. Get packed
    up and ready.

STORYTELLER: She told them where the station was.
    But there just wasn't room for all the people who
    wanted to go. After a while the train didn't stop.
    Couldn't stand the sight of people standing there,

looking at them and asking questions without saying a word. There were times during the quiet part of the night when Harriet Tubman would sing to herself in a voice so low you could hardly make out the words:

TUBMAN:
My people came to me
And said:
Harriet Tubman, lift your head.

It's time, they said,
We lived like men
It's time we stood up straight again.

Tired of tears
And bitter bread
Time we tried to laugh instead.

I raised my head
And said to them
Brothers, it's a hard thing to be men.

This we know,
They said to me
But we will not live in slavery
We will not live in slavery.

STORYTELLER: Friend Levi sat in the cab, his eyes looking ahead as though staring into the future. Mr. Garrison shoveled coal without stopping, as though a fire built hot enough would burn out the curse of slavery. When they got to the end of the line, they overhauled the engine and checked the firebox. Then they started back North. Once in the plantation country, they stopped traveling during the day. At night they'd keep going, trying to move without noise. It was a hard job, with the old engine wheezing and the axles on the coaches creaking.

GARRISON: Slaveholders and patrollers would have to be stone deaf not to hear this train.

TUBMAN: It will be worse when we're loaded. We have reservations for a hundred times more passengers than we have room for.

COFFIN: Where are we going to put them all?

GARRISON: We'll make room for them even if we have to take the roofs off the coaches.

TUBMAN: We'll be getting to the station soon.

STORYTELLER: Engineer Levi let the engine coast along for a while. Harriet Tubman, standing by him, pulled the whistle cord. The sound spread all over the land, low and strong.

TUBMAN: Sounds as if it's calling the whole world.

STORYTELLER: They listened, and as the sound of the whistle died away, the echoes came clear, and the trees rustled with it, and the crickets fiddled the sound of it. And a stir and a whisper like a million people waiting on the station platform was heard.

GARRISON: Sounds as if the whole world has got word about our train.

TUBMAN: Word gets around. It always does . . .
You can't keep the word from
   getting around
When everybody listens for the word
   to sound
And the word's in the sea, in the
   ground, in the air
And the free wind's blowing it
   everywhere.

People passing on the road say "Hello,
Say, friend, did you hear the
   free wind blow?
Say, friend, did you listen to

the wind and the sound?
Seemed to me it was saying:
  the word's going round!"

No, you can't keep the word from
  going round
When everybody listens for the
  word to sound
And the word's in the sea, in the
  ground, in the air
And the free wind's blowing it
  everywhere.

STORYTELLER: Friend Levi looked out, a big smile on his face, and watched the people climb into the coaches.

TUBMAN: The train's full, Levi. Not a bit of room anywhere. Passengers are standing in the aisles and sitting in the baggage racks. Let a few more on and there won't be room for you and Mr. Garrison.

STORYTELLER: She sings out . . .
All a-b-o-a-r-d
The Abolition Flyer
Shovel the coal
Push the steam up higher
Wheels a'rolling
Rolling along
And the whistle blowing
That freedom song.

PASSENGERS:
Got my ticket
On the Liberty Line
Leaving whip and chain behind.
Sing Hallelujah
Shout Amen
We get on slaves
And get off men.

STORYTELLER: Mr. Garrison shoveled coal and Friend Levi turned the throttle loose. The engine picked up steam and began to pound down the road a mile a minute. Everybody was smiling and feeling pretty good at the way that old engine was going. Suddenly, BANG—she stopped dead. Everybody stuck their heads out of the windows and yelled . . .

PASSENGERS: What's the trouble? Why are we stopping?

STORYTELLER: Far off they could hear the slavers' hound dogs baying. All the people—except the old ones and the children—got off the train, got behind it and pushed. They had a hard time getting her started, but they pushed her right up to Smoky Mountain. As soon as they got to the grade, she wouldn't move an inch. They'd push her ahead a bit, stop to catch their breath, and she'd slip right back.

GARRISON: Blast this blasted engine and this blasted mountain and the blasted slaveholders and their Congress and the Fugitive Slave Law and the Dred Scott Decision and Daniel Webster!

STORYTELLER: The sound of the baying hounds came closer and the children on the train began to cry.

GARRISON: No use. We need a lot more people than we have here to get this train over the mountain. It would take a majority of the people in the United States and the territories.

TUBMAN: Well, how about John Henry?

PASSENGERS:
Why, John Henry!
He's a man
Can do what a majority of people can.

TUBMAN: That's right. Get a majority of the people, and you can do pretty near anything.

PASSENGERS: And so can John Henry!

GARRISON: Get a majority of the people, and you can take this mountain and set it smack down in the middle of the Hall of Congress.

PASSENGERS: And so can John Henry!

COFFIN: Well, why don't we call him?

PASSENGERS *(Chanting in low tones at first, then increasing in volume):* J-o-h-n H-e-n-r-y . . . J-o-h-n H-e-n-r-y . . .

STORYTELLER: All of a sudden, everything was quiet, so quiet you could hear a noise like a big wind tearing the gound and the trees began to shake in the wind. The people looked up, and . . .
They saw a black man stand
As high as the mountain
With a hammer in his hand.

JOHN HENRY:
I'm John Henry.
They've been telling me
This road you're running
Rides my people free.

TUBMAN:
Oh, John Henry
I'm glad you could come.
We have to climb this mountain
Before the morning sun.

STORYTELLER: John Henry looked up and looked back. He saw the slavers behind him and the mountain ahead.

JOHN HENRY: It would take too long to climb the mountain with that old engine. And the roadbed's not much good. It's about time we got this stretch of road fixed. You all start pulling up that old spur on top of the mountain, and get the rails all piled up down here. We'll lay the rail underground . . .

Won't have trouble,
No grade to climb
Lose no passengers
On the Underground Line.

STORYTELLER: Then John Henry said to his hammer . . .

JOHN HENRY:

Lookit, old hammer
What you got to do:
Chop a hole through this mountain
Let liberty through.
Now, all you people
Better clear the track.
Once this hammer gets swinging
Mountain's liable to crack.

STORYTELLER: John Henry took one look around to see if everything was clear. He spit on his hands, hefted that hammer, and . . .

The earth it rolled
For ten miles under.
Mountain split
With a crack of thunder.
And it howled and it roared
And it stormed and it hailed
And the masters trembled
And the slave men quailed.
And people were saying . . .
What can that be?
Sounds like an earthquake—
Must be John Henry!

While John Henry was hammering through that mountain, the passengers were pounding out the roadbed and laying the rails. Fastest job of laying a roadbed you ever saw. And solid. That roadbed's better than a hundred years old now, but it's good as new. Fact is, it gets stronger every time somebody rides over it. The sun came up over the horizon, and the fog of slavery was lifted off the land. Harriet Tubman stood there waving to Friend Levi in the cab and Mr. Garrison shoveling coal. And the slave-catchers came into sight.

PASSENGERS: Get the engine started, Engineer Levi!

JOHN HENRY: Now, just take it easy. I'll push her to get you started.

STORYTELLER: John Henry took a running start, put both hands up against the back of the train, and pushed. That train shot down the grade into the tunnel as though shot from a cannon! The people on the observation platform shouted . . .

PASSENGERS: Much obliged, John Henry!

STORYTELLER: Their voices got fainter and fainter in the distance. Well, after that, of course, it was easy enough to expand that railroad. The Smoky Mountain stretch was always the best on the whole line. That's because President Levi Coffin got John Henry to be superintendent of the line!

THE END

Crispus Attucks

by Aileen Fisher

Born a slave—but who knows when?—
a fugitive from ruthless men,
Crispus Attucks made his way
to join a ship in Boston's bay.

He sailed the seas—who knows how long?—
this black man, young and tall and strong,
and then in a historic year*
it was his fate to reappear.

He walked with others of the crew
along the waterfront he knew,
and sensed a tension in the air:
"Why are these redcoats everywhere?"

"They're thrust upon us," townsfolk cried.
"We pay a tax that stings our pride.
We may not trade the way we please.
The English force us to our knees."

To Crispus Attucks, born a slave,
the colonists seemed less than brave.
And when the soldiers struck a lad,
he cried with all the voice he had:

"The way to get your freedom back
is not to grumble, but *attack*.
Come, follow. We've a stand to take
with rocks and clubs, for freedom's sake."

The redcoats flashed their bayonets
and shots rang out to still the threats.
Men fell before the rifle-burst,
and Crispus Attucks was the first . . .

The first to die in freedom's cause,
protesting England's stamp-tax laws,
the first to die for liberty,
before the war that made us free.

———

*1770

128

Arthur Ashe: Tennis Champion

by Mary Satchell

Characters

ARTHUR ASHE, *as young boy and man*
KEN ⎫
JOEY ⎬ *his friends, as youngsters and men*
WILSON ⎭
TOMMY
COACH, *basketball coach*
RONALD CHARITY, *college student*
MR. ASHE, *Arthur's father*
MRS. PRICE, *dorm supervisor*
DAVID ⎫
BOB ⎬ *teen tennis players*
PAUL ⎭
REPORTERS, *four or more, male and female*
ANNOUNCER, *offstage voice on microphone*
TWO MEN
DOCTOR
JEANNE, *Arthur's wife*
EXTRAS, *boys 7 to 12*

SCENE 1

TIME: *Summer, 1950.*

SETTING: *Basketball court. Sign reads,* BROOKFIELD PARK-RICHMOND, VIRGINIA. *Basketball net is center. Large box filled with sports equipment, including basketball, badminton racket, and birdie, is downstage.*

AT RISE: COACH *enters, a whistle around his neck. He moves to box, gets basketball, stands near net.* KEN, JOEY, WILSON, TOMMY, *and several other boys aged 7 to 12 run on and ad lib noisily while wrestling and roughhousing.*

COACH (*Good-naturedly*): O.K., guys. Let's get some order here. (*Boys keep playing.*) Break it up! (*Blows whistle; boys quickly form a line.*)

KEN (*Saluting*): Reporting for duty, Coach.

JOEY: Yeah. Just sign us up for the Brookfield Park peewee basketball team.

WILSON (*Quipping; cockily*): We don't need to try out for the team, Coach. You know we're the best.

COACH (*Chuckling*): Since you're so sure of yourselves, let's see what you can do with this. (*Tosses ball to boys, who begin playing while* COACH *watches.* ARTHUR *runs in, waving and shouting.*)

ARTHUR: Hey, Coach! Can I try out for your basketball team? (*Boys stop playing to stare at* ARTHUR.)

COACH (*Surprised*): What's your name, kid?

ARTHUR: Arthur Ashe, Jr.

COACH (*Studying* ARTHUR's *small frame*): How old are you, Arthur?

ARTHUR: Six, but I'll be seven on the tenth of July.

COACH (*Adjusting his cap*): You're pretty young.

ARTHUR: I'm almost as old as Joey. (*Points to* JOEY)

COACH: Arthur, things can get pretty rough out here. These guys are a lot bigger than you are.

ARTHUR (*Confidently*): I'm not scared of them, Coach. I can run fast and jump high. (*Eagerly*) Can I try out?

BOYS (*Ad libbing*): Aw, go on home. You're too weak to pick up a basketball. (*Etc.*)

ARTHUR: Please, Coach. Just give me a chance.

COACH (*Giving in*): All right, let's see what you can do. (*Points*) You guys, give Arthur some room and we'll see how he shoots baskets. (*Boys move to sidelines and ARTHUR takes ball, tries to shoot and misses several times. Boys snicker each time ARTHUR misses net.*)

WILSON (*Pretending*): Oh, Coach, please help! We can't stand to watch anymore. *Get him off the court!* (*Boys howl with laughter.*)

COACH (*Blowing whistle*): All right. That's enough. (*Boys quiet down.*) You guys could take a few lessons from this kid.

KEN: What kind of lessons?

COACH (*Putting hand on ARTHUR's shoulder*): Lessons in being good sports. Arthur's willing to try even though the odds may not be in his favor. It's his kind of spirit that makes a champion.

JOEY: That kind of spirit can make a guy a *pest*. (*Boys ad lib agreement. WILSON runs toward box.*)

COACH: Hey, Wilson! What are you doing? (*WILSON returns with badminton racket and birdie.*)

WILSON (*Giving racket and birdie to ARTHUR*): Here, maybe you'll have better luck hitting this birdie.

KEN (*Snickering*): Badminton may be too rough for him.

COACH: You've had your laugh, but something tells me Arthur may have the last laugh. (*Points off*) I'll meet you guys at the center in a few minutes for soft drinks and snacks. (*Boys cheer and run off;* ARTHUR *looks dejected.*) Don't mind them, Arthur. There are other sports besides basketball. I'm sure you'll find the one that's just right for you. Believe me, with your spirit, you're bound to be a winner. (COACH *exits;* ARTHUR *studies racket, then gives birdie a hard whack; it sails offstage.* ARTHUR *exits, carrying racket. Curtain*)

* * * * *

SCENE 2

TIME: *Several weeks later.*

SETTING: *Tennis court. Net stretches across stage. Downstage is folding chair with towel on it. Upstage is tall fence. Sign from Scene 1 remains in place.*

AT RISE: RONALD CHARITY *is lobbing tennis ball against fence.* ARTHUR *enters and watches until* RONALD *turns.*

RONALD (*Smiling*): Hey, I've seen you around here at the park a lot. (*Jokingly*) You must live at Brookfield.

ARTHUR: I do. (*Proudly; points*) My daddy is the park guard, and we have a house right over there.

RONALD (*Amused*): Well, that explains it. What's your name?

ARTHUR: Arthur Ashe, Jr. You must like to play tennis. Every time I see you, that's what you're doing.

RONALD: I think tennis is the greatest sport in the world. (*Wipes face with towel*) It's a rough, demanding sport that requires a lot of stamina.

ARTHUR (*Puzzled*): What's stamina?

RONALD: Strength and endurance.

ARTHUR: I'm strong. (*Points to racket*) Could you teach me to play?

RONALD (*Doubtfully*): You're kind of young, but maybe . . . (*Shakes* ARTHUR's *hand*) My name's Ronald

Charity. I'm a student at Virginia Union University and I teach tennis here at the park—part time.

ARTHUR: Pleased to meet you, Mr. Charity. Will you teach me to play right now?

RONALD (*Chuckling*): Slow down, Arthur. It takes a while to learn to play a good game of tennis. (*Hands racket to* ARTHUR) Let's see if you've got what it takes. (*Points to fence;* ARTHUR *runs upstage and gives ball a wallop against fence.* RONALD *whistles, impressed.*) Not bad! . . . You really want to learn how to play?

ARTHUR (*Eagerly*): I sure do!

RONALD (*Nodding*): Meet me here in an hour, and we'll start with some fundamentals of the game.

ARTHUR (*Happily*): Great! I'll be right on time!

RONALD (*Getting gear; moving to exit*): See you later. (*Turns*) Oh . . . you can keep this ball and racket. Bring them with you to practice.

ARTHUR: Thanks! (ARTHUR *takes equipment and* RON-ALD *exits.* ARTHUR *swings racket;* JOEY *and* KEN *enter with baseball bats.*)

JOEY: Hey, Art! We've been looking all over for you.

KEN (*Impatiently*): You're late for practice.

ARTHUR: Hi, guys. I guess I forgot all about the time.

KEN (*Pointing*): What are you doing with a tennis racket? Don't you know that tennis is a sissy sport?

ARTHUR (*Defensively*): No, it's not.

KEN: The guys will laugh if they see you with that.

ARTHUR (*Shrugging*): That won't bother me.

JOEY: Tennis is a long way from football, basketball, or baseball. Those are *our* sports, Art.

KEN: Most Negroes don't even play tennis. (MR. ASHE *enters, wearing security guard uniform; boys turn.*)

JOEY: Hey, Mr. Ashe. See if you can talk some sense into Art.

MR. ASHE (*Pleasantly*): Hello, Joey. Hi, Ken. (*To AR-THUR; amused*) What have you done to upset your friends, Arthur?

JOEY: Aw, he's got some crazy idea that he wants to play tennis, Mr. Ashe. (*Frowning*) Why would he want to do that?

KEN: Hey, Joey, we'd better get over to the field. Coach won't like it if we're late.

JOEY (*To* ARTHUR): Are you coming with us?

ARTHUR (*Shaking head*): Can't make it today, Joey. Mr. Charity's giving me a tennis lesson this afternoon.

KEN (*Exasperated*): You're wasting your time, Art.

JOEY: Yeah. Throw that tennis racket away, and get a baseball bat! (*Boys exit.*)

MR. ASHE: Your friends were rather hard on you, son.

ARTHUR: Joey and Ken never like anything they don't understand. (*Eagerly*) I think I'm going to like tennis, Dad.

MR. ASHE: Arthur, Jr., I'm proud of you and your positive spirit. You're not afraid to try something new. I don't know very much about tennis, but, if you really want to learn the sport, I'm behind you one hundred percent! (*He watches as* ARTHUR *takes a swing with tennis racket. Curtain*)

*   *   *   *   *

SCENE 3

TIME: *1960.* ARTHUR, *now 17, is already a champion tennis player.*

SETTING: *Inside cabin at a tennis camp. Two bunk beds are neatly made. Suitcases are on or beside three of the beds. Desk with lamp, chair, and two small bu-*

reaus are upstage. Easy chair, floor lamp, and rug are downstage. Wastebasket is near exit, left. Small bench is right, on apron.

AT RISE: ARTHUR, *carrying suitcase and tennis racket, enters with* MRS. PRICE, *who wears a suit and holds a clipboard.*

MRS. PRICE: This is where you'll be staying, Arthur.

ARTHUR (*Glancing around room*): Thanks, Mrs. Price. It looks as if my roommates have already checked in. (*Setting down suitcase*)

MRS. PRICE (*Nodding*): Some of the best young tennis players in the country are competing in our tournament this year. (*Pausing*) I should warn you, Arthur. Some people may resent your being here. You're the only Negro participating.

ARTHUR: Mrs. Price, my dad and I had a long talk before I came here. Dad told me just to keep my mind on playing tennis. He said I shouldn't worry about anything else.

MRS. PRICE (*Cheerfully*): That's the spirit, Arthur. You're a very level-headed boy for your age. (DAVID *enters, wearing eyeglasses.* ARTHUR *and* MRS. PRICE *turn.*) Hello, David. Arthur, this is David Allen. He'll be one of your roommates. David, (*Gestures*) this is Arthur Ashe, from Richmond, Virginia.

DAVID (*Friendly*): Hi, Arthur. (*Shakes* ARTHUR'S *hand*) Pleased to meet you. (*Points*) I've staked claim to this bunk. Paul and Bob were here first, so they get to sleep on the bottom beds.

ARTHUR: That's fine with me. (*Puts tennis racket and suitcase on a top bunk*)

MRS. PRICE: I'll get back to my office. See you boys later. (ARTHUR *and* DAVID *ad lib goodbyes as* MRS. PRICE *exits.*)

DAVID (*Sitting in easy chair*): So you're from Virginia. I've never been there.

ARTHUR: It's a nice place, but I'm not home very much these days. I travel around a lot to tennis tournaments. (BOB *and* PAUL *enter; stop in surprise.*)

BOB (*In hostile tone; gesturing to* ARTHUR): What's he doing here?

DAVID (*Rising quickly*): Hi, guys. (*Nervously*) This is Arthur Ashe. He'll be living with us during the tournament.

ARTHUR (*Holding out hand to* PAUL): Pleased to meet you.

PAUL (*Ignoring* ARTHUR'S *hand*): When did they start letting Negroes play in our tournament? (ARTHUR *opens suitcase; unpacks.* BOB *follows* ARTHUR *to bureau, watching him place clothes in empty drawer.*)

BOB (*Taunting*): I didn't know they had tennis courts in *their* part of town. (ARTHUR *continues to unpack, ignoring remarks.*)

DAVID: Come on, Arthur, I'll treat you to a Coke.

ARTHUR (*Nodding*): O.K. I'll finish unpacking later. (*Closes suitcase and exits with* DAVID. BOB *kicks wastebasket over.*)

BOB: He's got some nerve, acting like he belongs here! And we have to live with him, too!

PAUL (*Angrily*): No, we don't! I say we tear up this place. (*Knocks over lamp;* BOB *eagerly joins in, opening* ARTHUR'S *drawer and throwing clothes on floor. They pull bedspreads off beds, smash pictures, turn over chairs, rip pillows and scatter stuffing.* ARTHUR *and* DAVID *enter carrying sodas. They stop in their tracks.*)

ARTHUR (*Shocked*): What happened?

DAVID (*To* BOB *and* PAUL): Who did this?

BOB (*Flippantly*): Who do you think?

ARTHUR: But, why? It's crazy.

PAUL (*Shouting*): Who are you calling crazy?

DAVID (*Moving between* ARTHUR *and* PAUL): Arthur's right. (BOB *shoves* DAVID, *whose eyeglasses fall on floor.* PAUL *deliberately steps on glasses, smashing them.* ARTHUR *moves to defend* DAVID. MRS. PRICE *enters, followed by* REPORTER *with camera.*)

MRS. PRICE (*Horrified*): *Look at this cabin!* (*Indignantly*) Whoever did this won't take part in the tournament. I'll make sure of that!

REPORTER (*Gleefully*): Boy! And this was supposed to be a routine story. (*Takes pictures of room*)

MRS. PRICE (*Glaring at boys; coldly*): Who's responsible for this? (BOB *and* PAUL *glance secretly at each other, then point to* ARTHUR. MRS. PRICE *faces* ARTHUR, *does not see* BOB *and* PAUL *silently shake their fists and frown at* DAVID.) Is that true, Arthur?

ARTHUR: No, ma'am. (*Points to* BOB *and* PAUL) They did it. (*Turns quickly*) David can tell you the truth. (*All turn to* DAVID, *who glances fearfully at* BOB *and* PAUL.)

MRS. PRICE (To DAVID; *solemnly*): Did Arthur tear up this cabin? (DAVID *bows his head; refuses to speak.*)

ARTHUR (*Moving closer to* DAVID): Tell Mrs. Price the truth, David. (DAVID *turns his back to* ARTHUR. BOB *and* PAUL *secretly smirk in triumph.*)

MRS. PRICE (*Sighing*): It's obvious that David doesn't wish to accuse a boy he wants to be his friend. (*Turns to* ARTHUR) Some members of the tournament committee said that allowing a Negro to take part would be a mistake. (*Pauses*) I am sad to have to admit that they may be right.

ARTHUR (*Forcefully*): Mrs. Price, you're making a big

mistake. (MRS. PRICE *glances again at* DAVID, *who remains motionless, head bowed.*)

MRS. PRICE (*Pausing thoughtfully; then speaking decisively*): This reporter's here to interview the players for the local newspaper. (*To* DAVID, BOB, *and* PAUL) You boys go with him to the recreation hall, and we'll move you to another cabin before dinnertime.

REPORTER (*Snapping* ARTHUR's *picture*): What a story! Wait till my editor hears about *this*. (*Exits with* BOB, PAUL *and* DAVID)

ARTHUR (*Anxiously*): Are you going to call my dad?

MRS. PRICE (*Nodding*): I'll have to call him right away. (*Sadly*) Needless to say, Arthur, I hate to break this news to your father. (*Exits.* ARTHUR *moves slowly to pick up his clothes, which he packs. He then gets racket, sits dejectedly in easy chair. Lights fade to black. Curtain*)

* * * * *

SCENE 4

TIME: *Several hours later.*

SETTING: *Outside cabin. May be played before curtain.*

AT RISE: ARTHUR *enters with suitcase and tennis racket, sits on bench.* MR. ASHE *enters.*

MR. ASHE (*Calmly*): Hello, Arthur, Jr.

ARTHUR: Hello, Dad.

MR. ASHE: Mrs. Price has told me her side of what happened this morning in your cabin. Now, I want to hear what you have to say. (*Sits next to* ARTHUR)

ARTHUR (*Quietly*): I didn't do it, Dad. Two guys named Bob and Paul were responsible. I wasn't even in the room when it happened.

MR. ASHE: Did anybody else see what happened?

ARTHUR: David knows the truth. He and I were at the

center buying Cokes while Bob and Paul were tearing up the cabin.

MR. ASHE: What did David tell Mrs. Price?

ARTHUR (*Shaking his head*): Nothing. He's scared of the other guys, I guess. Nobody here believes me. (*Pauses*) Do you believe me, Dad?

MR. ASHE (*Studying* ARTHUR): Yes, I believe you. I know you well enough to know when you're telling me the truth. (*Places hand on* ARTHUR's *shoulder*) Let's go home, son.

ARTHUR: Dad, this will be in all the newspapers.

MR. ASHE: Don't worry, son. (*Firmly*) I know the truth, and that's all that matters. (*Picks up suitcase and racket*) There'll be other tournaments, and I want you to be ready for them. (*Gives racket to* ARTHUR)

ARTHUR (*Smiling*): Thanks for believing in me, Dad. (*They exit. Curtain*)

* * * * *

SCENE 5

TIME: *1965.*

SETTING: *Newspaper stand. Wastebasket and bench are nearby.*

AT RISE: TOMMY, *now in his twenties, is arranging papers.* MR. ASHE *enters.*

MR. ASHE (*Smiling*): Hello, Tommy. I haven't seen you since Arthur went off to college.

TOMMY (*Surprised*): Mr. Ashe! How have you been? (*They shake hands.*) Wow! Art's been named the best college tennis player in the U.S. (*Picks up magazine*) How does it feel to see your son's picture on the cover of *Sports Illustrated?*

MR. ASHE (*Proudly*): It feels great, Tommy.

TOMMY (*Giving magazine to* MR. ASHE, *who puts hand*

in his pocket to fish out money): Oh, no, this one's
on me.

MR. ASHE (*Chuckling*): Thanks, Tommy, but one's not
enough. (*Gestures happily*) I'll have to buy every
Sports Illustrated you've got so I can give them to all
my friends! (*Lights out. They exit. Spotlight up on*
Arthur, *poised for action in tennis togs. Banner*
reads, SPORTS ILLUSTRATED, 1965—ARTHUR ASHE,
NUMBER 1 AMATEUR TENNIS PLAYER. *Lights show*
ARTHUR *in silhouette.* ARTHUR *power-swings racket.*
Amplified sound of ball smashing against racket;
crowd applauds. Lights out. Singing of "We Shall
Overcome" is heard offstage. Spotlight on REPORTER
interviewing ARTHUR.)

REPORTER: Arthur Ashe, you're the first black American to be a member of the U.S. Davis Cup team. What
do you think is most important about your experi-
ences with the team?

ARTHUR: I hope that my being on the Davis Cup team
will send the world a message about race relations.
Our country's been torn apart by race riots. People
in other countries hear a lot of negative press about
racial problems in the U.S. But when they *see* black
and white tennis players being good friends and working well together, it *must* do some good. (*Lights out,*
then spotlight on ARTHUR's *silhouette, power-serving*
an imaginary ball. Sound: racket smashing ball.
Blackout. Spotlight on MEN *arguing.*)

1ST MAN: Arthur Ashe *was* a good tennis player. No
doubt about it. But he's thirty-one now, past his
prime.

2ND MAN: I wouldn't be so sure about that. I predict
he'll win at Wimbledon this year.

1ST MAN (*Incredulously*): Arthur Ashe beat Jimmy

Connors, the number-one tennis player in the world? Why, if that ever happened, I'd eat my hat! (*Lights out. Spotlight on* ARTHUR's *silhouette holding up racket in triumph. Crowd cheers. Lights out.* AN-NOUNCER *at mike, off.*)

ANNOUNCER (*Excitedly*): Arthur Ashe has just beaten twenty-two-year-old Jimmy Connors at Wimbledon! What a tremendous comeback! This day will certainly go down in tennis history. (*Spotlight on* DOCTOR, JEANNE, *and* MR. ASHE)

JEANNE (*Anxiously*): Doctor, how is my husband?

DOCTOR: His heart attack was quite severe, Mrs. Ashe. (*Shakes his head*) I don't like being the bearer of bad news, but your husband will never be able to play tennis again.

MR. ASHE (*Concerned*): I don't know how Arthur will take this news.

JEANNE (*With her hand on* MR. ASHE's *arm*): Arthur's very strong. He's a lot like you, Dad. He's always been eager to meet every challenge, and I know he'll overcome this one. (*Lights out. Silhouette of* ARTHUR *in coat and trousers, holding up large cup trophy.* ANNOUNCER *at mike, off.*)

ANNOUNCER: Arthur Ashe didn't let a heart attack stop him. Here it is 1982, and he's the captain and guiding force behind the winning U.S. Davis Cup team! Ashe has led his team to victory for the second consecutive year. This is truly Arthur Ashe's banner year! (*Applause; cheering. Lights out. Curtain*)

* * * * *

SCENE 6

TIME: *1985.*

SETTING: *Tennis Hall of Fame in Newport, Rhode Is-*

land. There is a platform with several chairs and po-
dium with mike opposite rows of chairs for audience.
Large banner reads, TENNIS HALL OF FAME—
INDUCTION CEREMONY FOR ARTHUR ROBERT
ASHE, JR.

AT RISE: ARTHUR *and* JEANNE *enter.*

JEANNE (*Excitedly*): Arthur, I'm so proud of you! Isn't
it wonderful?

ARTHUR: I can hardly believe it, Jeanne.

JEANNE (*Proudly*): People will be saying a lot of good
things about you today. (*Teasing him*) You're not going to let it go to your head, now, are you?

ARTHUR (*Chuckling*): Jeanne, you know me better
than that!

JEANNE (*Hugging him*): I'll be especially happy to know
that all the great things they're saying about you are
really true. (KEN, JOEY, WILSON, *and* TOMMY, *as men
dressed in suits and ties, enter.* WILSON *carries attaché case.*)

WILSON (*Cheerfully*): Hey, Art! I'll bet you never ex-
pected to see our faces again.

ARTHUR (*Surprised and pleased*): Is that really you,
Wilson? (*Incredulously*) Ken and Joey, too?

JOEY (*In deep voice*): It's *Joe* now, Arthur. I decided that
Joey had to go after I became a high school principal.
(ARTHUR *and friends ad lib happy reunion, hugging,
shaking hands, backslapping.*)

KEN (*Pointing to banner*): You made it, Arthur. The old
Brookfield Park team is very proud of you.

ARTHUR: This is a great day for me! (*Takes* JEANNE's
hand) Meet my wife, Jeanne. (*Friends ad lib greetings and shake her hand.*)

WILSON: We came early, hoping that we could have our
own ceremony for you, Art.

ARTHUR: What kind of ceremony?

KEN (*Jokingly*): A "last-laugh ceremony" might be one way to describe it.

JOEY: We just want to reminisce for a little while.

WILSON (*To* ARTHUR): I'll bet you didn't know you've had a fan club that's kept up with you all these years.

JEANNE (*Beaming*): See, Arthur? Today is even more special than we thought.

WILSON (*Gesturing*): Take a seat, Jeanne, and we'll get started. (JEANNE, KEN, JOEY, *and* TOMMY *sit in front row seats.* WILSON *points* ARTHUR *to a chair on platform, opens case, takes out scrapbook and small box, speaks into mike.*) We are here to honor Arthur Ashe, Jr., who wanted to be on our basketball team at Brookfield Park over 35 years ago. Art didn't make our team back then, though he tried hard. But he's had some successes that I'd like to share now. (*Reads*)

In 1960, Arthur was the youngest champion of the American Tennis Association. That same year, he received a tennis scholarship to UCLA.

In 1964, he received the Johnston Award, which goes to the tennis player who contributes most to the ideals of good sportsmanship.

In 1966, the city of Richmond, Virginia, held "Arthur Ashe Day." At one time, Art had not been allowed to play on the all-white tennis courts in that city.

In 1968, Arthur became the first black man to win a Grand Slam tournament at the U.S. Open in Forest Hills, New York.

In 1975, Arthur became the number-one tennis player in the world for the second time.

In retirement, Arthur has committed his life to the struggle for civil rights of black people in the U.S.,

South Africa, Haiti, and other parts of the world. (*Dramatically*) And today, Arthur will be inducted into the U.S. Lawn Tennis Hall of Fame. (*Turns to* ARTHUR) We salute you, Arthur, for your sports achievements, and for your inspirational life. (AR-THUR *rises; moves to podium.* WILSON *opens small box.*) Our old coach at Brookfield Park was right. We laughed at you on that basketball court, but now, *you've got the last laugh.* (*Brookfield friends rise.*) Arthur, it is our sincere pleasure to make you an honorary member of the Brookfield Park peewee basketball team of 1950. I gave you a badminton birdie on the day you tried out for our team, and today, I'm giving you another one—but this one is *solid gold.* (*Gives gold birdie to* ARTHUR, *who is deeply moved. All applaud.* REPORTERS *with cameras enter.*)

1ST REPORTER: Mr. Ashe, would you mind answering a few questions for us?

ARTHUR: Not at all. (*Moves to mike; others sit.* REPORT-ERS *get writing pads and pens ready; others position cameras.*)

1ST REPORTER: Mr. Ashe, what influences in your life would you say helped you become a tennis champion?

ARTHUR: There are three things that have greatly influenced my life in tennis. (*Smiles at* JEANNE) First is my family: my wife Jeanne and my daughter Camera. Second is my father's faith in me, (*Pauses*) and third, my friends from Richmond who are here today. I'm grateful to them for helping me become a success. (*Friends react with surprise, smile.*) They taught me that I had to perform well or get off the court. Through the years, whenever I felt discouraged, I thought about that day in Brookfield Park, and I'd get right back in the game. I promised myself that I'd

never give up. (*Holds up birdie*) And I never will!
(REPORTERS *take pictures. Applause. Curtain*)

* * * * *

EPILOGUE

TIME: *1997.*

SETTING: *Podium with mike is set before curtain. Banner reads,* ARTHUR ASHE STADIUM, FLUSHING MEADOWS, NEW YORK. *A bouquet of red roses is in front of podium.* JEANNE *enters, moves to podium.*

JEANNE (*Facing audience; speaking into mike*): Arthur would be very happy to know that this new stadium has been named in his honor. During his life, Arthur overcame many obstacles, and he had many accomplishments . . . as a tennis champion, a civil rights activist, a writer, husband, and father. (*Pauses*) Arthur's most difficult challenge came in 1988, when he discovered he was HIV positive. He contracted the virus through blood transfusions during surgery. Some people would have been defeated by this, but my husband never gave in to any kind of defeat. In 1992, Arthur established the Arthur Ashe Foundation for the Defeat of AIDS. The Foundation's objective is to help conquer AIDS on a global level through research and education. The Arthur Ashe Foundation and the Arthur Ashe Stadium are wonderful memorials to my husband's career and to his courageous life. (*Proudly*) I believe that our world is a much better place because Arthur Ashe has been a part of it. (*Applause, off.* JEANNE *exits.*)

THE END

PRODUCTION NOTES

ARTHUR ASHE: TENNIS CHAMPION

Characters: 14 male; 2 female; 6 or more extras, male or female, for Announcer, Doctor, and Reporters; as many extras as desired for 7- to 12-
year old boys.

Costumes: Coach wears athletic clothing, whistle around neck, and cap.
Boys, including Arthur, dress appropriately for sports practice; Ronald
wears tennis clothes. Mr. Ashe wears security guard uniform; Mrs. Price
wears suit and holds clipboard. David wears eyeglasses. In Scene 5,
Arthur wears tennis togs. In Scene 6, Ken, Joey, Wilson, and Tommy
wear suits and ties.

Setting: Scene 1, Basketball court. Sign reads, BROOKFIELD PARK—
RICHMOND, VIRGINIA. Basketball net is center. Large box filled with
sports equipment is downstage. Scene 2, Tennis court. Net stretches
across stage. Downstage is folding chair with towel on it. Upstage is tall
fence. Sign remains. Scene 3, Inside cabin at tennis camp. Two bunk
beds are neatly made. Suitcases on or beside three of the beds. Desk
with lamp, chair, and two small bureaus are upstage. Easy chair, floor
lamp, and rug are downstage. Wastebasket near exit, left. Small bench
is right, on apron. Scene 4, Outside cabin, played before curtain. Scene
5, Newspaper stand. Wastebasket and bench are nearby. Scene 6, Tennis
Hall of Fame in Newport, Rhode Island. There is a platform with several
chairs for audience. Large banner reads, TENNIS HALL OF FAME—
INDUCTION CEREMONY FOR ARTHUR ROBERT ASHE, JR. Epilogue, Podium with mike is set before curtain. Banner reads, ARTHUR ASHE STA-
DIUM, FLUSHING MEADOWS, NEW YORK. A bouquet of red roses is in
front of podium.

Properties: Tennis ball and racket; tennis bag for Ronald; baseball bats;
suitcase; sodas; reporters' camera, pads, and pens; newspapers and mag-
azines; banner reading, SPORTS ILLUSTRATED, 1965—ARTHUR ASHE,
NUMBER 1 AMATEUR TENNIS PLAYER; attaché case, with scrapbook and
small box.

Lighting: Lights fading; spotlights; blackout, as indicated in text.

Sound: Sound of ball smashing against racket.

Music: Singing of "We Shall Overcome."

I Have a Dream

by Aileen Fisher

Characters

JEFF
SUSAN
GRANDFATHER
SAMUEL
OTHER AUDIENCE MEMBERS
M.C.
BUS DRIVER
MRS. ROSA PARKS
BUS PASSENGERS
POLICE OFFICER
MARTIN LUTHER KING
BLACK MEN AND WOMEN
DALTON
COREY
CHORUS, *6 or more male and female*
STAGEHANDS
MARCHERS
LOUDSPEAKER VOICE

BEFORE RISE: *Music of "We Shall Overcome" is played in background as several audience members enter from back of auditorium and go to front rows to take seats.* JEFF *and* SUSAN *enter, carrying on conversation.*

JEFF: Until we studied about Martin Luther King in school, I never realized what a difference he made to this country.

SUSAN *(Nodding)*: He was a great man. I'm glad the school is honoring his birthday with this program. *(Looks around for seats)* Jeff, here are two good seats together. *(They sit.* GRANDFATHER *and* SAMUEL *enter at back of auditorium, start walking toward front.)*

SAMUEL: Where do you want to sit, Grandpa?

GRANDFATHER: Thanks to Martin Luther King, Samuel, we can sit any place we please. We black folks couldn't always do that.

SAMUEL: I know. We were considered second-class citizens, weren't we? When I hear you and Grandma talk about it, I wonder why it was like that.

GRANDFATHER: That's what Martin Luther King was always wondering—and asking. And he did something about it—something that changed the whole country. He reminded everyone that people in the United States should all have the same chance. That's what the Constitution says—"with liberty and justice for all."

SAMUEL *(Pointing to two seats)*: Let's sit right here, Grandpa. *(Lights dim.)* The program's about to begin.

*   *   *   *   *

SETTING: *Stage is bare. M.C.'s stand is at one side of stage. At the other side are two rows of chairs, angled so that they face the audience. A large sign reading* RESERVED FOR WHITES *is placed near the chairs in front. Chairs at the back have sign reading* COLORED SECTION. *A single chair for Bus Driver is placed in front of the two rows. On the backdrop is a large picture of Martin Luther King. If available, slides of*

*Martin Luther King and activities in which he was
engaged may be flashed on the backdrop from a projector throughout the play.*

AT RISE: *Spotlight goes up on M.C.'s stand. M.C. enters
and addresses audience.*

M.C.: We are gathered here today to celebrate the birthday of a great American—Martin Luther King—who
made a lasting impression on our history in his short
life of 39 years. Actually, his career as a leader in the
freedom movement didn't begin until he was 26 years
old. Before that his life ran smoothly enough. He went
to college, received a doctorate in theology, married,
and became pastor of a Baptist church in Montgomery,
Alabama. But on a December night in 1955, something
happened that changed the direction of his life. Picture
a crowded bus in the city of Montgomery, carrying
passengers home after a busy day. (BUS DRIVER *enters, sits in single chair. BUS PASSENGERS enter and
sit in chairs—white passengers in front section, blacks
in back section. Spotlight goes up on chairs. BUS
DRIVER pantomimes driving for a few moments, then
stops. More PASSENGERS enter, pay fare to DRIVER,
and take seats. MRS. ROSA PARKS, a black woman
carrying heavy bags, enters, pays fare to DRIVER,
then looks wearily at the chairs—mostly filled except
for one in front section. She sits there.*)

PASSENGER (*Angrily; to* ROSA): You'll have to move to
the back of the bus, lady. (ROSA *doesn't move.*) Can't
you read? (*Points to* RESERVED FOR WHITES *sign*)
These seats are for whites only. (DRIVER *looks
around, gets up, and goes over to* ROSA.)

DRIVER: Lady, these seats are reserved. Go to the back
of the bus where you belong. (ROSA *doesn't move or
speak.*)

OTHER WHITE PASSENGERS *(Ad lib):* She won't move!
Doesn't she know she can't sit in the front of the bus?
(Etc.)

DRIVER *(Angrily):* All right, lady. You asked for it.
(Steps to center stage, calls off) Officer! Officer, would
you come here, please? (OFFICER *enters.)*

OFFICER: What seems to be the problem?

DRIVER *(Pointing to* ROSA): This lady is the problem.
She won't move to the back of the bus.

OFFICER *(To* ROSA): You won't move, eh? *(Grabs her
arm, pulls her out of chair)* Then you're under arrest.
(He drags ROSA *off. Light goes out on chairs.* DRIVER
and PASSENGERS *exit;* STAGEHANDS *remove chairs
and signs. Spotlight goes up on* M.C.)

M.C.: For years black people in Alabama and other
southern states had been treated as if they had no
rights. If they complained, they were put in jail. White
people made the rules, and black people were ex-
pected to follow them. But the arrest of Mrs. Parks
aroused the black community in Montgomery to join
together and do something. They turned to their pastor, Martin Luther King, for help. (MARTIN LUTHER
KING, COREY, DALTON, *and several* BLACK MEN *and*
WOMEN *enter, stand center stage.)*

1ST MAN: Reverend King, we have to fight against this
injustice.

1ST WOMAN: What happened to Rosa Parks is a disgrace.
We've all suffered enough from white people's laws.

COREY: Let's take action—now! Not next week or next
year!

OTHERS *(Ad lib; angrily):* Yes, that's right! Let's fight!
(Etc.)

KING *(Holding up hand for silence):* I agree the time has
come to act. But we must do it peacefully, not with

meanness and violence. Excited talk blocks common sense, and the only way for us to fight unjust laws is to unite against them. We have to fight injustice with words and nonviolent action instead of clubs or guns.

DALTON: Reverend King, I have an idea. What if we all boycott the buses—walk to our jobs and have our children walk to school, instead of riding in the back of the bus.

2ND WOMAN: But my job is five miles away! I can't walk that far twice a day!

KING: Dalton has a good idea. (*To* 2ND WOMAN) You could find a ride with someone who has a car. Anything but ride the bus. If we all unite to boycott the buses, then maybe the white men who make the laws will change those laws!

OTHERS (*Ad lib*): Maybe a boycott could work! Yes, let's try it. (*Etc.*)

KING: But always remember the boycott must be orderly, and peaceful. No threats, no fighting, no violence. We're not doing this out of hatred of the white men, but to make them see that our cause is just.

COREY: That's right, Reverend King. We're tired of being mistreated, tired of being kicked about. It's time to act, but in a peaceful way! When will the boycott start?

KING: Tomorrow morning! Let's spread the news to our brothers and sisters, and remember to impress upon them the importance of nonviolence. "He who lives by the sword shall perish by the sword." (KING *and others exit. Spotlight goes up on* M.C.)

M.C.: The very next day, December 5, 1955, the boycott began. Bus after bus clattered down the street with no black passengers. Bus after bus, day after day, for months—until finally, the law was changed and blacks could sit anywhere on a bus, not only in Montgomery, Alabama, but in other cities and states as well. (MAR- TIN LUTHER KING *enters and crosses to center stage. Spotlight comes up on him.*)

KING: At last the words of our Declaration of Indepen- dence are beginning to have some meaning! "We hold these truths to be self-evident—that all men are cre- ated equal; that they are endowed by their Creator with certain inalienable rights; that among these are life, liberty, and the pursuit of happiness."

M.C.: Other words, bold words, mighty words, were written into the preamble to the Constitution of the United States:

KING: "We the people of the United States, in order to form a more perfect Union, establish justice, insure domestic tranquillity, provide for the common defense, promote the general welfare, and secure the blessings of liberty to ourselves and our posterity. . . ." (KING *exits. Spot up on* M.C.)

M.C.: Martin Luther King's work for liberty had just begun. In many states, particularly in the South, white children and black children were not permitted to go to the same school; black children could not play in public parks. Many restaurants had signs in their windows: COLORED NOT WELCOME. One by one, Mar- tin Luther King tackled the issues, driven on by his dreams of justice, and more and more black people looked to him for leadership. Meanwhile, Reverend King was put in jail again and again for his uncom- promising stand on equality. His house was bombed. Still, his faith never wavered. (CHORUS *crosses back- stage, singing first stanza of "We Shall Overcome.")*

CHORUS: We shall overcome
      We shall overcome

We shall overcome some day.
Oh, deep in my heart
I do believe
We shall overcome some day.

M.C.: Then came August, 1963, one hundred years after Abraham Lincoln issued his Emancipation Proclamation freeing the slaves. With the blessing of Martin Luther King, more than 200,000 people, black and white, took part in a "march for jobs and freedom" and gathered at the Lincoln Memorial in Washington, D.C., where Dr. King gave his famous "I Have a Dream" speech. It was carried in newspapers all over the country. (KING *enters, crosses center. Spotlight goes up on him.*)

KING: I have a dream that my four little children will one day live in a nation where they will not be judged by the color of their skin but by the content of their character.

I have a dream today.

I have a dream that one day the state of Alabama will be transformed into a situation where little black boys and black girls will be able to join hands with little white boys and white girls and walk together as sisters and brothers.

I have a dream today. . . .

And if America is to be a great nation this must become true. So let freedom ring from the prodigious hilltops of New Hampshire! . . .

Let freedom ring from every hill and mole hill of Mississippi. From every mountainside, let freedom ring.

When we let freedom ring, when we let it ring from every village and every hamlet, from every state and every city, we will be able to speed up that day when

all of God's children, black men and white men, Jews
and Gentiles, Protestants and Catholics, will be able
to join hands and sing that old Negro spiritual, "Free
at last! Free at last! Thank God almighty, we are free
at last!" (*Exits*)

M.C.: Martin Luther King's success in promoting nonviolence as a solution to racial problems was recognized by the world in 1964, when he received the No-
bel Peace Prize. He was only 35 years old, the youngest person ever to receive the prize. All over the
world people watched on television as he accepted the
award of $54,000. He donated it to the civil rights
movement. (KING *enters; spotlight goes up on him.*)

KING: On behalf of all men who love peace and brother-
hood, I accept this award . . . with an abiding faith
in America . . . and a profound recognition that nonviolence is the answer to the crucial political and moral
question of our time. I have faith that one day, the
long night of racial injustice will be over. I still believe
that we shall overcome. (*Exits*)

CHORUS (*Singing offstage*):
        We'll walk hand in hand
        We'll walk hand in hand
        We'll walk hand in hand some day
        Oh, deep in my heart
        I do believe
        We'll walk hand in hand some day.

M.C.: The climax of Martin Luther King's career came
in the spring of 1965, with the 54-mile "right to vote"
march from Selma, Alabama, to Montgomery, the
state's capital. The 15th Amendment, ratified almost
100 years before the Selma march, gave blacks in this
country the right to vote, but blacks in some states
still couldn't vote, because they were not allowed to

register. Martin Luther King was determined to fight this injustice, but he faced bitter opposition in Alabama.

Hundreds of marchers of every faith and race started on the walk from Selma under a sweltering sun. They had gone only a few blocks when they were met by a blockade of state troopers swinging billy clubs and carrying canisters of tear gas. The marchers knelt down before the troopers, who pressed ahead, swinging their clubs with abandon and spraying the air with gas. Dr. King saw that there was nothing to do but retreat.

Two weeks later he tried again, this time leading 8,000 supporters on the march to the state capital. A federal court order was issued to protect the marchers, and National Guard troops were on hand in case of trouble. Five days later Reverend King and his fellow marchers arrived at the capitol building in Montgomery, where 25,000 people had gathered to welcome them. (KING *and* MARCHERS *enter, gather center.*)

KING: We are on the move! And we are not about to go back. We will go on, with faith in nonviolent action, for our cause is humane and just. It will not take long, because the arm of the universe bends toward justice.

MARCHERS (*Ad lib*): We will go on! (*Etc.*)

M.C. As a champion of peace, Martin Luther King opposed the war in Vietnam.

KING: We must work for peace by peaceful means. War is madness, and this madness must cease. (*Exits with* MARCHERS)

M.C.: For his outspoken views on this and many other national problems, Martin Luther King was continually in danger for his life. His family, too, suffered from threats, and several times the King home was bombed. In April, 1968, he went to Memphis to address striking sanitation workers. As usual his message was for peace, justice, and equality. No one was prepared for the violence that erupted. While Dr. King was speaking to a friend from the balcony of his motel, a shot rang out. Dr. King slumped to the floor. . . .

LOUDSPEAKER: Special news bulletin from Memphis, Tennessee! Martin Luther King has just been assassinated! We will supply more details as they come in. . . .

M.C.: Martin Luther King died just an hour after the shooting, a martyr to the cause of equality and peace. He was not yet forty years old. (*Music of "We Shall Overcome" is heard softly offstage.*) Yes, Martin Luther King had a dream, a dream for the future that will bring hope to the oppressed wherever they are, a dream to overcome injustice with fairness and equality. For as Reverend King said, the arm of the universe bends toward justice. (*Music swells. Curtain*)

THE END

PRODUCTION NOTES

I HAVE A DREAM

Characters: 8 male; 2 female; 1 male or female for M.C.; male and female extras for all other characters.

Playing Time: 20 minutes.

Costumes: Jeff, Susan, Grandfather, Samuel, Other Audience Members and M.C. wear modern, everyday dress. All other characters wear clothes appropriate for the 1950's and early 1960's.

Properties: Shopping bags for Rosa Parks.

Setting: Stage is bare. M.C.'s stand is at one side of stage. At other side are two rows of chairs, angled so that they face the audience. Large sign reading RESERVED FOR WHITES is near chairs in front. Chairs at the back have sign reading COLORED SECTION. Single chair for Bus Driver is in front of the two rows. On the backdrop is a large picture of Martin Luther King. If available, slides of Martin Luther King and activities in which he was engaged may be flashed on backdrop from a projector throughout the play.

Lighting: Spotlights, as indicated.

Music: "We Shall Overcome."